D1154625

Incest in Faulkner
A Metaphor for the Fall

Studies in Modern Literature, No. 55

A. Walton Litz, General Series Editor

Professor of English
Princeton University

Joseph Blotner

Consulting Editor for Titles on William Faulkner
Professor of English
University of Michigan

Other Titles in This Series

Incest in Faulkner
A Metaphor for the Fall

by
Constance Hill Hall

UMI RESEARCH PRESS
Ann Arbor, Michigan

Produced and distributed by
UMI Research Press
an imprint of
University Microfilms International
A Xerox Information Resources Company
Ann Arbor, Michigan 48106

Library of Congress Cataloging in Publication Data

Hall, Constance Hill, 1933-
Incest in Faulkner.

(Studies in modern literature ; no. 55)
A revision of author's thesis (Ph.D.)—Texas A&M
University, 1983.
Bibliography: p.
Includes index.
1. Faulkner, William, 1897-1962—Criticism and
interpretation. 2. Incest in literature. 3. Fall of
man in literature. 4. Sex in literature. I. Title.
II. Series.
PS3511.A86Z7843 1986   813'.52   85-20826
ISBN 0-8357-1712-7 (alk. paper)

For my family
Charles, Cynthia, Jim, Julie, and Martha

Contents

Acknowledgments

For their thoughtful and careful readings of the manuscript, I would like to express my appreciation to Stanley Archer, Garland Bayliss, Norman Grabo, Larry Reynolds, and especially to David Stewart who provided invaluable criticism and encouragement through many readings of the work. Gratitude is owing to Floyd Watkins for his comments and suggestions on earlier versions of chapter 2 of this book. My thanks go to Alfred Shivers for his recommendations and assistance and for the generosity with which he gave his time. I would like to acknowledge also the contribution of my sister-in-law, Judith Hill, whose encounters with incest in her legal practice first drew my attention to Faulkner's emphasis on it in his works.

Grateful acknowledgment is made to the following for permission to use quotations: Alfred A. Knopf for excerpts from Thomas Mann's *Death in Venice*, translated by Kenneth Burke; Random House for excerpts from the following Faulkner works: *Absalom, Absalom!*, *As I Lay Dying*, *Flags in the Dust*, *Go Down, Moses*, *The Hamlet*, *Sanctuary: The Original Text*, *The Sound and the Fury*; Chatto & Windus for excerpts from Faulkner's *Flags in the Dust*, *Go Down, Moses*, *The Hamlet*, *Sanctuary: The Original Text*; and Curtis Brown for excerpts from Faulkner's *Absalom, Absalom!*, *As I Lay Dying*, *The Sound and the Fury*.

Abbreviations

References to Faulkner's texts, noted parenthetically, are to the following editions:

AA *Absalom, Absalom!* [1936] New York: Random House, 1966.

AILD *As I Lay Dying.* [1930] New York: Random House, 1964.

FD *Flags in the Dust.* New York: Random House, 1973.

GDM *Go Down, Moses.* [1942] New York: Modern Library-Random House, 1955.

H *The Hamlet.* [1940] New York: Random House, 1964.

LA *Light in August.* [1932] New York: Random House, 1932.

M *Mosquitoes.* [1927] New York: Liveright, 1951.

S *Sanctuary.* [1931] New York: Vintage-Random House, 1967.

SOT *Sanctuary: The Original Text.* New York: Random House, 1981.

SF *The Sound and the Fury.* [1929] New York: Random House, 1966.

SFA Appendix, *The Sound and the Fury.* [1946] New York: Modern Library-Random House, 1967.

SP *Soldier's Pay.* [1926] New York: Liveright, 1951.

Uv *The Unvanquished.* New York: Random House, 1938.

WP *The Wild Palms.* [1939] New York: Modern Library-Random House, 1984.

1

Introduction

In the first half of the twentieth century and particularly in the Deep South, incest was still very much in the closet; in fact, at the time of Faulkner's writing, a discussion of incest was almost as taboo as the act itself. It is a theme, however, which pervades much of Faulkner's fiction. It emerges very early in his writing, in his second novel, *Mosquitoes,* and appears in a number of his books: *Flags in the Dust, Sanctuary, As I Lay Dying, Go Down, Moses, The Unvanquished, Pylon, The Wild Palms,* and *Knight's Gambit.* It is featured prominently in his two greatest novels: *The Sound and the Fury* and *Absalom, Absalom!* The persistence of such a theme attests certainly to its importance, but what is not made clear is why the writer included so insistently a topic that, particularly in his time, was viewed with repugnance and horror. It is a question which can best be answered, I believe, by viewing the problem from the perspectives of a variety of disciplines, by investigating the studies of incest in anthropology, psychology, history and literature. A survey of their findings should provide a general understanding of incest that elucidates Faulkner's intentions.

Anthropology concerns itself primarily with the origins and purposes of the incest taboo, a proscription that is found, anthropologists tell us, in almost every society and in virtually every period of history.[1] The taboo against sexual relations within the nuclear family has been particularly strong and has been almost universally observed. The attitude toward incest which occurs outside the immediate circle is less stern and varies from one society to the other; a few cultures have permitted half brothers and sisters to marry, or uncles and nieces, aunts and nephews, and even more have sanctioned the marriages of cousins. At certain periods in history, these exceptions have been extended to include even the incest of full siblings. Brother-sister marriages within the royal household were permitted in Egypt, Hawaii, Uganda, and the empire of the Incas; and in Egypt following the Roman conquest, the practice was adopted by the commoners of the country. On special occasions, also, incest has been sanctioned, particularly "in the context of magic and rituals," as a means of acquiring some coveted attribute, such as purity or courage.[2] Such exceptions, however, serve only to prove the rule; the rarity with which they appear and the interest which is generated accordingly attest to the universality and the effectiveness of the taboo. Its success has been such, in fact, that its importance to man and to his evolution cannot be ignored; it is considered by many anthropologists to provide the very key to our humanity—to mark "the breakthrough from nature into culture" and to be "the basic concept on which all human societies are founded."[3]

While most anthropologists agree on the universality of the incest taboo, they do not concur as to its origins or purpose; and theories proliferate on how and why the ban came into being. The first explanation, introduced in 1979 by L. H. Morgan, holds that consanguineous marriages were prohibited because they resulted in offspring that were physically and mentally defective. This theory, which was later discredited, has in recent years found new supporters, among them the psychologist Gilbert Lindzey; he maintains that natural selection favors the stronger and healthier groups which observe the taboo and are hence more fit, with the result that the incest ban is perpetuated in the surviving groups. Another possibility was put forward by Ernest Westermarck: the natural aversion theory, which holds that people reared together will not be attracted to one another sexually. It is a position which has been supported recently by Robin Fox, who argues that incest is not so much repressed as it is avoided, that this avoidance is instinctual rather than learned, and that the aversion is transmitted genetically. Freud's "quasi-anthropological" explanation of the taboo is contained in his Myth of the Primal Horde. According to this story, the sons of a primordial family murdered the tyrannical father who had kept them from the women of the family, but then, seized by remorse, they renounced those very women they had hoped to obtain. B. Malinowski advanced the theory that the incest ban was instituted to preserve the unity of the family and to ensure the proper development of the young, a notion that was later expanded and extended by Talcott Parsons. According to E. B. Tylor and subsequently L. A. White, the taboo originated in the need to "marry out" in order to survive—the necessity, that is, for the clan to encourage the marriages of its members with those of other groups, thereby enlarging its kinship circle and acquiring the protection that numbers afford. It is a theory which finds support in Margaret Mead's study of the Arapesh tribesmen, primitives who regard incest as a type of selfish hoarding and denial of the opportunity to expand one's family. Maintaining that no one theory can explain a taboo that is the result of a variety of causes, George Murdock takes a multidisciplinary approach that includes psychological, sociological, and cultural aspects of the problem. In a new and novel argument, Mariam Slater contends that the conditions of life in primitive times—the shorter span of the parents' lives, the higher rate of infant mortality, and the wider spacing in the births of children—all militated against the occurrence of incest and that the taboo, when it was introduced, served primarily to formalize a situation that already existed.[4]

In the eyes of the anthropologists, then, the purpose of the incest taboo is survival: it encourages the propagation of the species, the cohesion of society, the preservation of the family, and the integration of the individual. It is a view that is shared by Faulkner, who dramatizes in his work the disintegration and destruction that follows in the wake of the ban's violation.

While anthropologists concern themselves primarily with the matter of the taboo, psychologists tend to focus on the way incest functions in particular cases, on the questions of why it occurs and how it affects the people involved. They are interested not in theoretical but in practical considerations—the kinds and types of injuries it inflicts. This functional approach is evidenced in the psychologists' definition of incest, their expansion of it to include quasi-incestuous situations in which the damage incurred is similar to that in cases of true incest. This broader interpretation encompasses sexual activity which falls short of actual intercourse and also includes sexual relationships of people connected by adoption and marriage as well as blood.[5] The effectiveness of the taboo, psychologists note, increases in direct proportion to the amount of damage that is involved: mother-son incest, regarded with the greatest repugnance and also the most crippling, rarely occurs; the incest of siblings, which involves the least trauma, is probably the most common, although seldom reported; father-daughter incest falls somewhere in between, in regard to the frequency of its occurrence and the damage it involves.[6] As psychologists see it, then, the primary purpose of the taboo is the prevention of injuries; more specifically, it is the protection of the children of the family so that they can grow and mature and can eventually become self-sufficient and independent adults.

The causes of incest, as psychologists point out, are many and complex and may lie partially in the situation in which a family is thrust, but they are to be found primarily in the personalities of the participants themselves, in those traits and characteristics which apparently predispose them to the breaking of the taboo. As their psychological profiles reveal, incest offenders are usually very troubled people unable to cope with a family life that is often disrupted and fragmented. The incestuous father, generally, is a lonely and isolated man, a weak and dependent person who is at the same time arrogant, abusive, and violent with his family. Incest often appeals to him as an opportunity to express his hostility or to exercise his authority. He may drink excessively, and he is sometimes psychopathic, if not psychotic. Frequently, he is fixated on his mother, the symbol for him of unlimited love and affection, and he appears in the incestuous relationship to be in search of a surrogate for this earlier source of comfort. The incestuous daughter usually is very passive and dependent and, because she often assumes the housekeeping and child-rearing responsibilities, appears mature beyond her years. In cases of sibling incest, the brother and sister are likely to be shy and introverted people, the children of weak and neglectful parents who fail to provide a strong and positive influence. The part played by the mother is particularly significant. Typically, she is a person who is either passive and dependent or else rigid and puritanical; she usually is a mother who is not present to her family, often relinquishing her responsibilities to her daughter and sometimes abandoning her children altogether. The mother who is a partner in incest is frequently, like the incestuous father, a weak and dependent person, introverted and alienated; she too has often been fixated on the parent of the opposite sex and appears to be searching for warmth and affection. The personality of the incestuous son is notable chiefly for the severity of his emotional disturbance, which often borders on, and sometimes erupts into, schizophrenia.[7]

Incest, however, not only results from but also contributes to disintegration. There follows in its wake a multitude of disorders: depression, delinquency, suicidal tendencies, prostitution, frigidity and impotence, homosexuality, and multiple personalities. Sometimes the very causes become also the effects; the conditions which encouraged the incest—isolation or the abuse of drugs and alcohol or perhaps sexual promiscuity—are themselves aggravated and augmented by what they had promoted. Clearly, the consequences of incest are devastating; the family becomes more and more fragmented, and the participant displays increasingly an inability to function as a whole, healthy, and productive adult.[8]

Such is the case in Faulkner's fiction, where the incestuous characters (or those with tendencies in that direction) conform to a remarkable degree to the psychologists' profiles of incest offenders. This is not to say, however, that Faulkner was in any way influenced by the studies of psychologists. At the time of the writing of *Flags in the Dust, The Sound and the Fury,* and *Absalom, Absalom!*—the novels in which the incest theme is most prominent—very little had been written on the subject of incest.[9] And Faulkner himself has admitted to only a scant knowledge of psychology.[10] The compatibility of his portraits of incestuous characters with the psychologists' profiles can be explained instead by the keenness of his powers of observation and by his intuitive understanding of people and, perhaps, by an acquaintance with or a knowledge of violators of the taboo.[11]

While anthropology concerns itself primarily with the origins and ends of the incest taboo and psychology with clinical studies of incest offenders, history looks at the incidence of incest within the context of world events. Interested principally in the conflicts between man and the taboo, history records the efforts of man to evade, to ignore, to challenge, and to manipulate the taboo, and it notes also the instances in which the incest ban has dictated to man and to events.

Generally, man has not emerged the winner to his battles with the taboo, but in some periods of history and within a rather narrowly ascribed set of circumstances, the taboo has been abrogated and the practice of incest sanctioned. In ancient times, incestuous marriages within the royal family were permitted in a few Eastern countries, of which Egypt is perhaps the most notable. Consanguineous marriage appeared there first in the fourth dynasty (2700–2650 B.C.) and emerged again in the eighteenth (sixteenth century B.C.), but it was during the reign of the Ptolemies that royal incest was practiced with the greatest fervor. For a period of three hundred years, beginning with the marriage of Ptolemy II and his sister Arsinoe Philadelphia and ending with the death of the famous Cleopatra, wife to two full brothers, the Ptolemies adhered to the tradition. Under the rule of the Romans, which followed the Ptolemaic period, the custom of sibling marriage spread also to the common people of the country, where it persisted until 295 A.D., the date of its abolition by the emperor Diocletian. Two other Near Eastern countries of the ancient world that sanctioned royal incest were Persia and Caria, Persia in the third century B.C. and Caria in the fourth. In Persia, it is speculated, the marriages of the king Cambyses to two of his sisters may also have ushered in an era of institutionalized sibling marriages for all classes of Persians.[12]

Royal incest was also practiced in two countries of the Far East: Japan and Korea. It apparently was a custom of long duration in Japan, the period of its acceptance spanning the reigns of the country's first eighty emperors. Most of these incestuous unions consisted of the marriages of cousins or of uncles and nieces, aunts and nephews, but the incest of siblings appeared also in the royal genealogies, most notably in the reign of the nineteenth emperor and during the rule of the Soga dynasty. Royal incest was introduced in Korea during the dynasty of the Koryos when the second emperor of that clan married his sister and made her his empress, a practice which was continued by the two emperors who succeeded him to the throne. The purpose of the Koryos in instituting sibling marriage, a practice which was contrary to the customs of the country, was to stabilize and unify the dynasty by limiting the peripheries of a clan which had expanded too rapidly. It was a goal, in fact, which was shared by all the dynasties—in all countries and in every period of history—that practiced and promoted consanguineous marriage; in maintaining "the purity of the blood" and in keeping the domain within the family, they hoped to enable the dynasty to endure. In Korea, however, as in all the countries which sanctioned its practice, incest was a privilege that, with one or two exceptions, was reserved for royalty, and its incidence there was relatively rare.

With the exception of the Incas and the Hawaiians, none of the peoples of the Western world, however, have sanctioned incest. From the very beginnings of Western civilization, it has been regarded with a great deal of repugnance, so much so that not only the violation of the taboo but even the suspicion of its occurrence could wreck a career or destroy a dynasty. The ostracism of the Greek general Cimon in the fifth century B.C. was due in large part to his alleged incest with his sister, Elpinice. The flagrant incest of Gaius Caligula, Roman emperor of the first century A.D., with all of his sisters and particularly with Drusilla, appalled his subjects and contributed, certainly, to the end that he met at the hands of assassins.[13]

After the eclipse of Greece and Rome, the prohibitions against incest became entrenched more strongly than ever in the West. The increased horror of incest was due primarily to the Christianization of the Western world and to the severity with which incest was regarded within the Judeo-Christian faith. Incest was tolerated and even condoned, it is true, in certain instances in the Bible: the union of Adam and Eve, the marriages of their children, the incest of Lot with his daughters, Abraham's marriage to his half sister Sarah, and Tamar's incest with her father-in-law, Judah.[14] These occasions, however, occurred very early in the biblical history of man and were defended on the grounds that they were necessary to the survival of the race. With the promulgation of the laws of Moses, incest for Jews and Christians was unequivocally and forever condemned. In Leviticus and Deuteronomy, it was explicitly defined and forbidden, and in both the Old and New Testaments instances of incest were noted and censured.[15] The strength with which these injunctions took effect may well be evidenced in the birth and growth of Western monasticism, a movement which counted in its roster of founders and leaders an unusually large number of brother-sister pairs, including the father of Western monasticism, Saint Benedict of Nursia, and his twin sister, Scholastica.[16] What is suggested by the number and the prominence of these sibling pairs is that the vigor of these orders and perhaps the very fact of their existence may have owed something to the repression and sublimation of incestuous desires. If so, in this instance the church proved itself able not only to accommodate but to utilize the affections it had forbidden. The church, however, did not remain altogether free of the taint of incest. One of its popes, Alexander VI, was widely believed to have committed incest with his daughter, Lucrezia Borgia; the French clergy of the thirteenth century indulged so openly and flagrantly in incestuous behavior that they were forbidden by decree from sharing their dwellings with mothers and sisters.[17]

While the Roman Catholic Church remained unalterably opposed to incest, it refused, however, to countenance its use as a weapon in royal suits for divorce. Two kings who made this discovery for themselves were Lothar II of Lotharingia (Lorraine) and Henry VIII of England, who hoped to extricate themselves from marriages that had produced no heirs. The stories of their struggles involved multiple instances of incest, some of it rumored and some of it real. In his attempt to secure the succession, Lothar repeatedly accused his wife, Theutberga, of committing incest with her brother; yet at the same time, he found himself the ally of his incestuous cousin Judith, who had shocked all England with her marriage to her step-son Aethelbald. In his efforts to establish his line, Henry claimed that two of his marriages were incestuous, the first because Catherine was his brother Arthur's widow and the second because, previous to the marriage, he had taken Anne's sister as his mistress and hence stood as a brother-in-law in relation to her. To bolster his case against Anne, he accused her of incestuous conduct with her brother; it was rumored as well that Henry had been the lover of Anne's mother and was the natural father of Anne. Additionally, the marriage of Henry and Jane Seymour could be considered incestuous, for they were related within the forbidden fourth degree of consanguinity. In their efforts to perpetuate their dynasties, however, both kings were ultimately defeated. In his battles to have his marriage annulled, Lothar made no headway at all against the church; despite his many marriages, made possible only by a complete break with Catholicism, Henry did not get the heir he needed. In neither case did the succession endure beyond one generation, and in Lothar's case, the kingdom itself was destroyed.[18]

The sanctioning of incest, then, occurred for the most part in the Eastern hemisphere and in ancient times. In the Western world, particularly after its Christianization, the taboo against incest was vigorously enforced. In a few cultures, though, in both the East and the West, royal incest persisted until, relatively speaking, fairly recent times. However, when it collided with the attitudes of the more modern Western world, it too came abruptly to an end. In the middle of the sixteenth century, Spanish conquistadores condemned and halted the Incan practice of royal incest which had continued uninterrupted for ten generations. In the first quarter of the nineteenth century, American missionaries put an end to royal incest in Hawaii, a tradition on the island for approximately eleven generations. Early in the twentieth century, the incest which was practiced for six generations by the monarchs of Siam also ceased, largely as the result of the Westernization of its kings.[19]

We see, then, that in almost all cultures of the world and in most periods of history, the incest taboo was honored. Those cultures which sanctioned incest were only a handful among many; the privilege of incest was restricted almost always to royalty; and it was, relatively speaking, of limited duration. Those individuals who challenged the ban were usually embroiled in a tangle of dynastic politics and almost always went down in inglorious defeat. Faulkner's stories, which often feature characters suggesting historical figures, also record the defeat and demise of the clan when it collides with the incest taboo.

In its treatment of incest, literature in a sense incorporates the approaches of all three of the other disciplines under discussion. Like the psychologist, the writer of fiction is concerned with the working of the mind and heart of a particular person; like the anthropologist, he is interested in the theoretical implications that incest holds; and like the historian, he sees a particular act of incest expanded and enlarged by its relation to the figures and events of other times and places. The difference lies in the writer's interest in incest not only as a reality but also as a symbol, his concern with the multitude of directions in which incest points. He may interpret incest as a manifestation of "a desire to do evil," "the wish to revolt," or "a craving to engage in what may seem the most intimate of all possible unions." It may symbolize the preying of the past upon the present or the tyranny of authority. It can signify also alienation and isolation and be indicative of a narcissistic sensibility, a "predilection for solipsism." In some instances, when the incest is committed unknowingly, it may represent not only a moral evil but a metaphysical one as well, symbolizing an element of irrationality and perverseness in both the psyche and in the universe. Almost invariably, however, incest in literature denotes disaster; catastrophe follows in its wake.[20]

The theme of incest has been present in Western literature from its inception. It appears in Homer and is suggested in Aeschylus but becomes a major theme first in Sophocles' play, *Oedipus the King*. This great tragedy, from which the bulk of literary treatments of incest descends, is of course the starting point for any survey of incest in literature. In this drama, which focuses on the incest committed unknowingly by mother and son and which includes as well the acts of patricide, suicide, and self-mutilation, several important points are made: that the outcome of incest is always disaster; "that insidious lusts exist in the best and bravest of men"; "that there is an element of irrational caprice in the order of things."[21] Two other dramas of classical Greece which take incest as their theme are Euripides' *Aeolus* and the story of Byblus and her brother, both of them preserved, in part at least, in Ovid's *Metamorphoses*; although the protagonists in these stories yield to the incestuous impulse in full awareness of the blood relationship, one lesson remains the same, that incest culminates in catastrophe.

In the literature of the Middle Ages, not surprisingly, the incest theme was very seldom in evidence. During the period, however, the first complete prose account of Signy and Siegmund made its appearance in the *Volsungasaga,* a story in which the incest is justified, as it is in the Old Testament, on the grounds that it is necessary for the perpetuation of the race. Another medieval work which takes incest as a theme is Hartmann von Aue's *Gregorius von Steine,* a fictionalized account of the life of Gregory I, in which the pope is represented not only as the child of brother-sister incest but as an offender as well, a man who unwittingly marries his own mother-aunt. No sin, this strange tale seems to say, is so heinous that it cannot be forgiven; even the perpetrator of incest is capable of redemption.[22]

The Renaissance witnessed a resurgence of interest in incest as a literary theme. In the last half of the sixteenth century, Marguerite de Navarre offered another pseudo-biography of Gregory I, *A Tale of Incest,* which not only retains the incest found in earlier versions, that of mother-son and brother-sister, but includes father and daughter incest as well. In this rendition, where only the mother commits incest knowingly and she alone is punished, the message appears to be that the sin lies in the intent and not in the deed, a conclusion in marked contrast to that reached by Sophocles' *Oedipus.* Another Frenchman interested in incest was Rosset, who dealt with the brother-sister relationship in one of his stories from *Histoires tragiques de notretemps.* Incest is featured also in two children's stories of the period: "Penta the Handless" and "The She Bear," from Giabattista Basile's *The Tale of Tales for the Diversion of Little Ones.* In 1626 there appeared for the first time on the English stage a play that attacked the subject of incest openly and directly: John Ford's *'Tis a Pity She's a Whore.* Concluding with the deaths of the incestuous brother and sister, it demonstrates, like *Oedipus,* "the helplessness of man before the onsweep of fate."[23]

In the literature of the neoclassical period, the incest theme also appeared but only occasionally, and its presence there was considerably muted. Several redactions of the Oedipus story came out, among them the versions furnished by Corneille, by Voltaire, and by Dryden and Lee.

Dryden also deals with incest in *Don Sebastian* and *Love Triumphant*; the Comte de Sade writes of it in *The Philosophy in the Boudoir* and in *The Crimes of Love*; Henry Fielding in *Tom Jones* offers a humorous treatment of the theme.

In the Gothic works of the late eighteenth and early nineteenth centuries, which found the sensationalist aspects of incest admirably suited to their purposes, the incest theme enjoyed a revival of interest. In most of these novels and dramas, the incest is committed unconsciously, is ascribed to the capricious working of fate, and is met with a punishment that is sudden and severe. In the first of the Gothic dramas, Horace Walpole's *The Mysterious Mother*, the protagonist unknowingly marries a woman who is at once his sister and his mother; *The Monk*, a fin de siècle work by M. G. Lewis, describes the violations and murders of two women by a man who later discovers that the victims were his mother and sister.

The theme of incest flourished in the literature of the Romantic period. Of the many works treating incest at this time, the following are, perhaps, the most notable: *Mirra* and *Filippo*, by Vittorio Alfieri; *René*, by François-René de Chateaubriand; Schiller's *The Bride of Messina*; Goethe's *Brother and Sister* and *Wilhelm Meister*; *The Bride of Abydos* and *Manfred* by Byron; Shelley's *The Cenci* and *Laon and Cythna*; "The Fall of the House of Usher" by Poe; Hawthorne's "Alice Doane's Appeal"; Melville's *Pierre: Or the Ambiguities*. Sibling incest was the kind depicted most often in this period because it represented for these writers "the ultimate expression . . . of the tradition of courtly or 'romantic' love."[24] Like the lovers in the songs of the wandering troubadours or the tales of the court poets, these incestuous couples are marked by their obsession with love and the lover, by their proclivity for lamenting and for suffering, and by their tendency to seal themselves off from a disapproving world. In the literature of the Romantics, incest is usually committed consciously and deliberately and signifies not only alienation and isolation but narcissism as well. Usually, however, the writers treat the lovers sympathetically, and in some instances they go so far as to idealize the relationship.

The theme of incest continues to thrive in the literature of the twentieth century. In the preponderance of these works, the incest is committed unconsciously; in the tradition of Oedipus, the partners have long been separated and are therefore ignorant of the ties that bind them. Such works include Isak Dinesen's "The Caryatids," Edgar Saltus' *The Monster*, *Homo Faber* by Max Frisch, *Brothers and Sisters* by Ivy Compton-Burnett, and Edmund Keely's *The Libation*. In some twentieth-century works, however, the incest is committed knowingly and deliberately by a couple fully aware of their blood relationship. This is the case in Maugham's "The Book Bag," in Iris Murdoch's *A Severed Head,* Robinson Jeffers' "Tamar" and "The Tower beyond Tragedy," *The Velvet Horn* by Andrew Lytle, and Thomas Mann's "The Blood of the Walsungs." Also belonging to this second category are the works of William Faulkner, with the possible exceptions of *Absalom, Absalom!* and *Go Down, Moses;* even in these novels, however, each of the relationships in question contains one partner who knows of the family ties.

Unconscious incest, of course, would not appeal to Faulkner; it would not meet the needs of a concept that is indebted, I believe, to Milton's *Paradise Lost.* Both Milton and Faulkner conceive of incest as a metaphor for original sin.[25] Symbolic of a willful and arrogant defiance of God, incest in *Paradise Lost* is a conscious and deliberate act and one that has terrible consequences. Satan's incest with his daughter, the child of his apostasy, follows close on the heels of his rebellion and is a product of that revolt; it results in the birth of Death. This sin is compounded by that of Death's repeated rape of his mother, embraces that issue the monstrous "Hell Hounds," "hourly conceived / And hourly born."[26] Similarly, Adam's incest with Eve, his "daughter" and "consort," is the immediate result of their Fall and the "seal" of their disobedience.[27] By this act, the First Parents acquire carnal knowledge and call down upon themselves—and all posterity as well—the sentence of death. In Faulkner, too, we find evil and sin and death personified, Adamic and Eve-like creatures drawn. Here also the incest springs from pride, ambition, anger, and lust, from a sense of injured merit, and a desire for revenge. And here, moreover, the consequences are the same: the expulsion from Eden, a descent into brutehood and into bondage, the advent of suffering and death. Finally, we find that in Faulkner, also, the propensity to sin is bequeathed, and hence the cycle of fall and punishment is endlessly repeated.

Faulkner never acknowledged openly the obligation to Milton, but this omission in no way obviates the possibility of such a debt. A similar situation existed in relation to Eliot, whose influence upon Faulkner is marked and is often remarked. Moreover, we do know that Faulkner read Milton. He made a statement to that effect in Nagano; and according to Joseph Blotner, he owned two copies of Milton's works: *Complete Poetry and Selected Prose of John Milton,* which he kept at his home in Charlottesville, and *The Poetical Works of John Milton,* which remained in the library at Rowan Oak.[28] Most importantly, Faulkner's own work testifies to the influence which Milton exerted upon him. There appears in the novels and stories, particularly those from the extraordinarily creative years at the end of the twenties and in the thirties, a number of Milton borrowings in which the verbal resemblances are striking. In many instances, Faulkner refers specifically to Milton or to one of his works: in *Soldiers' Pay,* Januarius Jones takes a copy of *Paradise Lost* from the shelf in the rector's study, and Dr. Gary's preference of Milton over Swinburne is noted; in "The Leg" from *Collected Stories,* George recites for Everbe some passages from *Comus*; and in *Mosquitoes,* Dawson Fairchild, discussing the teaching of literature, mentions *Paradise Lost.* [29] In a scene in *Flags in the Dust* which hints that the Benbow's intimacy may have something to do with Milton, Narcissa seats herself on her brother's bed and listens to Horace intone, from the bath, the phrases of "Milton's archangels in their sonorous plunging ruin." [30]

Thus far, however, the possibility of a debt to Milton has received little critical attention. No book on the subject has been written and, with the exception of one brief note, no article has appeared. [31] Two of the Faulkner scholars most interested in Faulkner's sources, Michael Millgate and Richard Adams, make no mention in their writings of Milton; yet both affirm the importance to Faulkner of English and European literature, and both deplore the failure of critics to recognize and to record this influence on his art. [32] The affinities between Faulkner's work and Milton's have not, however, gone entirely unnoticed. Cleanth Brooks has drawn attention to the likeness which certain characters in Faulkner bear to those of Milton, and he has noted in *Flags in the Dust* the presence of a Milton borrowing, a phrase that echoes the wording of a passage from *Areopagitica.* Brooks has commented also on the compatibility of Faulkner's "theism" with Milton's version of Christianity, notably in his emphasis on the freedom of man's will and man's responsibility for his actions and in the stress on God's refusal to protect man from the devil and his assaults. [33] Olga Vickery has found some Miltonic echoes in Ike's long discourse on the sins of the South in *Go Down, Moses*; she draws attention particularly to the "emphasis on the hierarchy and the contractual agreement between man and God" and to the insistence on man's free will and on his responsibility, despite the foreknowledge of God, for his Fall. [34] Percy Adams finds Faulkner's concept of evil in the Snopes trilogy to be Miltonic; Albert J. Guerard takes note of the Miltonic elements in Faulkner's style; Vincent Hopper identifies the hubris of Sutpen with Satan's defiance of God. But only David Aiken, in his article on *The Sound and the Fury,* treats at any length the parallels between *Paradise Lost* and one of the novels under discussion here. [35] In a listing such as this, the comments may seem numerous, but they shrink in significance when regarded in the context of the Faulkner industry's enormous output. Additionally, these observations are never fully and adequately developed; they appear for the most part as brief asides and notations and, at best, are expanded to a paragraph or perhaps a page or two.

Although the subject of incest in Faulkner has unquestionably received more critical attention than the Milton connection, it too has been
largely ignored. In the book-length studies of Faulkner, the discussions
of incest usually are confined to a paragraph or two and are limited to
two works: *The Sound and the Fury* and *Absalom, Absalom!* Most often
they are directed toward the Compson family and focus on the psychology
of Quentin. In the effort to fathom what incest means to Quentin, the
critics posit a number of possibilities: an attempt to define "some point
beyond which surely no one would venture to transgress"; "a scheme for
regaining lost innocence"; an effort "to make Compson honor a thing of
importance and momentous significance even as he destroys it"; "a strat-
egy for attaining being by affirming the possibility of sin"; an attempt at
"rebellion and liberation"; the effort to prove the "significance of his
standard by violating it 'dreadfully.' "[36] A few critics delve briefly into
the significance of incest in *Absalom, Absalom!* Vickery maintains that
Henry sees in the incest evidence of a love "which will not be restricted";
O'Connor interprets "this desire for incest" as "an acceptance of defeat
and . . . doom," an acknowledgment of the "spiritual incest" already
committed by the South's white people in holding themselves apart from
the black.[37] Jenkins maintains that the Southern mentality equates incest
with miscegenation, seeing in both a threat to the "sanctity of the bloodline"; and he concludes that the abhorrence with which the white man
views miscegenation derives from his own similarly dark but repressed
incestuous desires.[38]

While David Minter reveals a greater interest than most in the subject
of incest, he gives it relatively little space and is concerned primarily with
its relationship to creativity. As he sees it, the creation of art serves for
Faulkner's characters and for Faulkner himself as a means of satisfying
and realizing repressed incestuous desires. The paintings of Elmer, in the
unfinished work of that name, serve as substitutes for "the impossible
and forbidden" relationships Elmer desires. Horace's art in *Flags in the
Dust* "is devoted to the imaginative possession of figures he is forbidden
and fears sexually to possess." This sublimation of incestuous impulses
enables both Elmer and Horace, however, to avoid Quentin's fate; they
can "achieve satisfaction . . . without arousing guilt." And, according to
Minter, this has been the case with Faulkner as well, particularly in the
writing of *The Sound and the Fury,* where his life and art, like Elmer's,
become "strategies of approximation."[39]

To date, the only book-length study of incest in Faulkner is John T.
Irwin's *Doubling & Incest / Repetition & Revenge: A Speculative Reading
of Faulkner,* a work that is narrowly Freudian and highly speculative.
Focusing primarily on *The Sound and the Fury* and *Absalom, Absalom!,*

Irwin maintains that the relationship between these two novels corresponds to that of a teller and the tale, a writer and his work, and that it represents an incestuous doubling whereby the artist hopes to conquer mortality and time. This relationship between the two books, according to Irwin, provides the key to the structure of Faulkner's best work; in the many doublings between the Compson and Sutpen families, one discovers a structure in which "the struggle between the father and the son in the incest complex is played out again and again in a series of spatial and temporal repetitions, a series of substitutive doublings and reversals. . . ." Faulkner, that is, is engaged in an oedipal struggle with his literary fathers, his predecessors, and this struggle is embodied in the character of Quentin. Furthermore, Irwin maintains that Faulkner's use of this metaphor for his art was conscious and deliberate and was present in his work from its beginnings.[40]

Just three articles address the topic of incest in Faulkner. In a brief *Explicator* item, Earle Labor argues that the knife scene in *The Sound and the Fury* implies a hysterectomy and not incest, as some have suggested. In another note, Marvin Morillo maintains that one of Shreve's comments contains a reference to Byron's *Don Juan,* which is meant to call attention to the poet's relationship with his half-sister and to underscore Quentin's commitment to the idea of incest. In the only full-length article to confront the topic, Robert J. Kloss provides a Freudian but helpful interpretation of *As I Lay Dying.*[41]

Other essays offer, occasionally, a few observations on the subject and, less frequently, advance a theory as to its significance in Faulkner's work. In a chapter from his book, Albert Guerard states that in Faulkner the "preoccupation with incest is connected both with a veneration of virginity and, less demonstrably, with a dread of normal intercourse"; in his article, John Arthos sees incest in Faulkner as a metaphor for original sin, as "the symbol of the original evil." Writing on *Flags in the Dust,* Kerry McSweeney maintains that "the incestuous element in the relationship of Horace and Narcissa" is "clearly related to their mutual longing for a life denying existence." According to Weatherby, incest in *Absalom, Absalom!* is perceived as an alternative to miscegenation, at least by Henry, who "chooses Bon for Judith, almost sensing the blood link between them." Maintaining that the relationship between Judith and Bon is symbolic of "ideal human intimacies of love within the family metaphor," Lensing states that Mr. Compson intuits in this relationship "a love so rare and strong . . . that the metaphor which can best describe it is that of incest." In a comparison of Jeffers' "Tamar" and *Absalom, Absalom!,* Beth Haury calls attention to the affinities between the two tales of incest, without however indicating what the significance of those affinities might be.[42]

The theme of incest is addressed most often in discussions of *The Sound and the Fury*. Carvel Collins, in "Miss Quentin's Paternity Again," refutes the theory posited by George R. Stewart and Joseph M. Backus that Caddy and Benjy were involved in an incestuous relationship. Dauner maintains that Quentin, in refusing to acknowledge his incestuous feelings for his sister, "denies his instinctual nature, which Caddy so intensely exemplifies."[43] In the eyes of some critics, Quentin's incestuous relationship with his sister is "historically representative," a symbol of "aristocratic decadence," or the decline of the Compsons, or the death of the South.[44] It is also regarded as "psychologically representative," a manifestation of the drives from within: the quest for identity, the desire for self-sufficiency and wholeness, the wish to escape the world of time and suffering, the effort to "transform meaningless degeneracy into significant doom," and the attempt to return to the innocence of childhood.[45]

In the mountain of criticism on Faulkner, then, we find little to facilitate our understanding of incest in his works. Relatively few comments appear at all; even fewer choose to elaborate on the topic; only occasionally is a general theory advanced. In just four instances is the subject of incest made the focus of the criticism: the book by Irwin and the articles by Kloss, Morillo, and Labor. It is a subject with many questions still unanswered.

2

Flags in the Dust

When Faulkner wrote his publisher, Horace Liveright, in October of 1927, concerning the manuscript he had just completed, he had no doubts as to its merits: " 'at last and certainly, as Orens' sheik said, I have written *the* book, of which those other things were but foals. I believe it is the damdest best book you'll look at this year, and any other publisher.' "[1] Liveright, however, did not share his enthusiasm for *Flags in the Dust*. According to Faulkner, he found it "chaotic, without head or tail," and friends who read the manuscript also said "the same general thing—that the book lacked any form whatever."[2] Nor have many critics since been favorably impressed with either *Flags in the Dust* or its edited version, *Sartoris*.

But *Flags in the Dust*, if not *Sartoris*, deserves a better reception. This version of the novel, longer than *Sartoris* by a fourth, opens up rich new ground for an interpretation of the first novel in the Yoknapatawpha cycle—the germ of Faulkner's apocrypha.[3] In restoring the excised segments, material dealing primarily with the Benbow family and particularly the relationship of Horace and Narcissa, it accomplishes an important shift in focus: Horace's role is better delineated; added weight is given to the Benbow section so that it balances that of the Sartoris family; and most important, the incestuous nature of the brother-sister attachment is made more apparent.

An understanding of this relationship, in turn, throws new light on the novel as a whole: it illuminates the concept of the duality of man; it elucidates the function of the other characters and relationships in the book; it clarifies and supports the theme of the oppression of the past. As we have already noted, in Faulkner incest serves as a metaphor for the Fall. This function is suggested in the scene of Horace's homecoming, where Narcissa sits on her brother's bed as Horace intones, from the bath, the phrases of "Milton's archangels in their sonorous plunging ruin" (*FD*, 154). As a metaphor for the original sin, incest signifies a fall from wholeness, a lapse in which mind is sundered from body, thought from sensation. Rarely are the two halves of man's nature in equilibrium; thought represses feeling, and feeling exacts its revenge.[4] This contest is dramatized in the divided souls of the stories' characters. The major figures are depicted as one or the other of the bifurcated parts; the lesser characters function as their mirrors or foils, reflecting and revealing the hidden dark corners of the protagonists' hearts. The theme of incest in the Benbow sections is closely related to the theme of the past in the Sartoris segments. Both reveal an unhealthy preoccupation with the idea of family, signifying, in their separate ways, an intensification and distortion of the love of kin. Each represents also an aspect of the Fall. In the Sartoris pride is found the seed of Satan's and Eve's rebellion; in the incest of the Benbows, the first consequence of the original sin. Incest in *Flags in the Dust* points also in other directions. It springs from and leads to a variety of disorders: repression, division, regression, narcissism, and the drive to destruction. These are disorders that describe not only Horace and Narcissa but also the world in which they live; they are easily recognized as aspects of the twentieth-century malaise.

The many ramifications of Horace's and Narcissa's relationship are perhaps captured best, certainly most graphically and succinctly, in their symbolic representation in the Benbow garden. It is the scene of Horace's homecoming, and he views the house and garden for the first time since his departure for Europe and World War I:

> The meaning of peace. They turned into an intersecting street narrower but more shady and even quieter, with a golden Arcadian drowse, and drove through a gate in a honeysuckle-covered fence of iron pickets. From the gate the cinder-packed drive rose in a grave curve between cedars. The cedars had been set out by an English architect of the 'forties, who had built the house (with the minor concession of a veranda) in the funereal light Tudor which the young Victoria had sanctioned; and beneath and among them, even on the brightest days, lay a resinous exhilarating gloom. Mockingbirds loved them, and catbirds, and thrushes demurely mellifluous in the late afternoon; but the grass beneath them was sparse or not at all and there were no insects save fireflies in the dusk.
>
> The drive ascended to the house and curved before it and descended again to the street in an unbroken arc of cedars. Within the arc rose a lone oak tree, broad and huge and low; around its trunk ran a wooden bench. About this halfmoon of lawn and without the arc of the drive, were bridal wreath and crepe-myrtle bushes old as time, and huge as age, would make them. Big as trees they were, and in one fence corner was an astonishing clump of stunted banana palms and in the other a lantana with its clotted wounds, which Francis Benbow had brought home from Barbados in a tophatbox in '71.
>
> About the oak and from the funereal scimitar of the drive, lawn flowed streetward with good sward broken by random clumps of jonquil and narcissus and gladiolus. Originally the lawn was in terraces and the flowers constituted a formal bed on the first terrace. Then Will Benbow, Horace and Narcissa's father, had had the terraces

obliterated. It was done with plows and scrapers and the lawn was seeded anew with grass, and he had supposed the flower bed destroyed. But the next spring the scattered bulbs sprouted again, and now every year the lawn was stippled with bloom in yellow, white and pink without order. Neighbors' children played quietly beneath the cedars, and a certain few young girls asked and received permission to pick some of the flowers each spring. At the top of the drive, where it curved away descending again, sat the brick doll's house in which Horace and Narcissa lived, surrounded always by that cool, faintly-stringent odor of cedar trees.

It was trimmed with white and it had mullioned casements brought out from England; along the veranda eaves and above the door grew a wistaria vine like heavy tarred rope and thicker than a man's wrist. The lower casements stood open upon billowing curtains of white dimity; upon the sill you expected to see a scrubbed wooden bowl, or at least an immaculate and supercilious cat. (*FD.* 151–52)

It is a description which calls to mind another landscape, the surreal terrain which appears in Thomas Mann's novella, *Death in Venice.*[5] In Part One, immediately following his encounter with the stranger in the mortuary portico, Aschenbach experiences a kind of seizure, a hallucination which transports him to a jungle-like scene:

He saw a landscape, a tropical swamp-land under a heavy, murky sky, damp, luxuriant and enormous, a kind of prehistoric wilderness of islands, bogs, and arms of water, sluggish with mud; he saw, near him and in the distance, the hairy shafts of palms rising out of a rank lecherous thicket, out of places where the plant-life was fat, swollen, and blossoming exhorbitantly; he saw strangely misshapen trees lowering their roots into the ground, into stagnant pools with greenish reflections; and here, between floating flowers which were milk-white and large as dishes, birds of a strange nature, high-shoulders, with crooked bills, were standing in the muck, and looking motionlessly to one side; between dense, knotted stalks of bamboo he saw the glint from the eyes of a crouching tiger—and he felt his heart knocking with fear and with puzzling desires.[6]

The impression which this scene made on Faulkner's imagination is not felt in *Flags in the Dust* alone. It is even more apparent in *Mosquitoes,* where the "fecund" swamp surrounding Lake Pontchartrain recalls Mann's marshland in countless details: the shimmering heat and the absence of sound, "the huge gaudy bird," "foul sluggish" water, "implacable sky," "rank" and "monstrous" grass, the "dark streams"—"aimless and obscene," the "huge cypress roots thrust up like weathered bones out of a green scum," "the bearded eternal trees"—"thick" and "huge," the landscape's air of a prehistoric scene, the "yearning" in David's eyes and the heavy beating of his heart. (*M,* 169–213). Associated with sex not only in its imagery but also by its reputation as a trysting place for the lustful locals, this tropical setting provides an appropriate backdrop for the abortive elopement of Pat and David.

The many borrowings from *Death in Venice* which appear in the recently published *Elmer,* an unfinished novel written in 1925, also argue for the Mann influence on Faulkner.[7] The high esteem in which Mann was held by Faulkner points too in that direction. Faulkner owned copies of *Buddenbrooks* and *Stories of Three Decades* (which contains *Death in Venice*), and in both volumes he inscribed his name, a mark of his fondness for a work.[8] In an interview in Japan, he made specific mention of *Death in Venice,* and on a number of occasions, he expressed the opinion that Mann was one of the greatest writers of his time.[9] Additionally, a connection between *Death in Venice* and *Flags in the Dust* is hinted, it seems, in Horace's reference to Venice as he talks to Narcissa: " 'Venice. A voluptuous dream, a little sinister. Must take you there some day.' "[10]

Although the landscape in *Flags in the Dust* is far less flamboyant than those in either *Mosquitoes* or *Death in Venice,* it resembles them not only in imagery but also in function. It too reveals an interior terrain, exposing emotions which have long been repressed and which threaten to erupt in distorted and sinister forms; and it also adumbrates much that will occur later in the story.

The salient feature of Faulkner's garden, like Mann's, is the sexual suggestiveness of its imagery, which points, in *Flags in the Dust,* to Horace's and Narcissa's incestuous love. The Benbow lawn contains bridal wreath, the myrtle (flower of Aphrodite), honeysuckle and wistaria (the honeysuckle clearly linked to sexual desire in *The Sound and the Fury,* the wistaria to thwarted love in *Absalom, Absalom!*). What is suggested in the imagery appears to be confirmed in the relationship. There is, first of all, a physical intimacy that is unusual between siblings. Horace strokes Narcissa's face and her knee; Narcissa rests her hand on her brother's knee and clamps his arm against her side. Her gesture at Thanksgiving dinner, when she reaches under the table and squeezes his knee, recalls Mann's incestuous twins, Siegmund and Sieglinde of "The Blood of the Walsungs," holding hands at dinner "between their chairs."[11]

Even more convincing is the verbal evidence, the number of telling statements made by the Benbow pair. Narcissa declares that she is glad she has Horace "instead of one of those Sartorises"; she maintains that she "wouldn't have treated Horace that way," that is, that she would not have left him as he left her; she observes that men cause only unhappiness and that, as much as she loved him, she "couldn't keep Horace" (*FD,* 151, 193, 245). On his part, Horace expresses the hope, in Part Four, that Narcissa has "come home for good"; and he confesses regret at having "exchanged her for Belle" (*FD,* 287). We have also the comments of other characters: Miss Jenny's observation to Narcissa that Horace was making an old maid of her but that now (now, that is, that Horace has taken up with Belle) she can get married; and Bayard's garbled, confused, and unwitting but highly significant statement, made in a bar in Chicago: "Wife used to be wife's brother's girl" (*FD*, 355). It is Belle, however, who puts the problem plainly: " 'you're in love with your sister. What do the books call it? What sort of complex?' "[12]

A number of images associated with Horace and Narcissa also carry sexual implications, particularly the bell, which the bell-shaped narcissus links with Narcissa. It appears in Horace's pleased contemplation of the life he resumes following his return from the war:

> The meaning of peace, he said to himself again, releasing the grave words one by one within the cool bell of silence in which he had come at last again, hearing them linger with a dying fall pure as silver and crystal struck lightly together. (*FD*, 157)

In a similar passage, which replaces the "bell" with a "vessel" and ties the image more closely to Narcissa, Horace inveighs against his sister's decision to marry Bayard:

> Suddenly he began to speak at her with thin fury, watching the sense of his words accomplish steadily behind her eyes, a half sentence behind, as though he were pouring them from a distance into a vessel. (*SOT*, 17)

Narcissa's identification with the vessel in this passage recalls Horace's association of her with the urn, an object well-known as a sexual symbol. In *Light in August*, where Joe Christmas envisions a row of "suavely shaped" but imperfect urns, the significance of the urn is quite clear: "Each one was cracked and from each crack there issued something liquid, deathcolored, and foul."[13] Similar images of corruption, linked also with sex, are associated with Horace and Narcissa in *Sanctuary*, where Horace recalls a scene from his childhood: "he and Narcissa paddled and splashed with tucked-up garments and muddy bottoms" in a rain-drenched street, "a canal of blackish substance half earth, half water" (*SOT*, 10). The appearance of the muddy bottom in this passage anticipates its use in *The Sound and the Fury* as a symbol of Caddy's fall; the "blackish substance" calls to mind the corruption that flows, in *Sanctuary*, from Madame Bovary's mouth; the canals may have a reference to the disease-infested waterways (and souls) of *Death in Venice*.

Suggestions of incest are also found in the identification of the poetical Horace with Lord Byron, the English Romantic whose love affair with his half-sister Augusta is a well-known and well-noted piece of literary lore. In a letter to Narcissa, Horace writes, "and I'd be sad that I couldn't be everywhere at once, or that all spring couldn't be concentrated in one place, like Byron's ladies' mouths" (*FD*, 339). This passage, as Marvin Morillo points out, undoubtedly alludes to one in *Don Juan*

(VI.xxvii), "in which Byron in an excess of osculatory greediness wishes all women's mouths one mouth."[14] In his note on *The Sound and the Fury,* Morillo contends that a similar allusion in that book is meant to direct the reader's attention to Byron and his sister and hence to underscore Quentin's incestuous love for Caddy. The same purpose is served in *Flags in the Dust.* In "There Was A Queen," moreover, Narcissa is linked similarly with Byron when she describes for Aunt Jenny the anguish that Byron Snopes's letters have caused her:

> "When Bayard and I were on our honeymoon, I was wild. I couldn't even think about him alone. It was like having to sleep with all men in the world at the same time."[15]

This parody associates Narcissa with the British poet and his incest not only in its allusion to *Don Juan* but also in the reference to Snopes, who bears Byron's name and also represents aspects of Horace's personality. It is no accident, certainly, that the man who is so passionately and obscenely in love with Narcissa bears the name Byron; nor is it coincidental that references to Narcissa's letters from him frame the emotional scene that takes place in *Flags in the Dust* between Horace and his sister in Narcissa's bedroom.

However, the forbidden promptings of the Benbows' hearts, like Aschenbach's in *Death in Venice,* have been rigorously repressed, a condition suggested again by the garden's imagery: the "clump of stunted banana palms," the "lantana with its clotted wounds," the Tudor-Victorian architecture of the house, and the inclusion not of a tiger but a cat.[16] This element of repression is deeply ingrained in the Benbows' relationship; for Horace's and Narcissa's attraction to one another, which is itself repressed, results from the sublimation of oedipal desires for the parent.[17] This is suggested, first of all, by Narcissa's assumption of the role of surrogate mother. Even before Julia Benbow died, this shadowy and withdrawn figure had been supplanted by Narcissa, who had established so firmly her maternal control that "by the time she was five or six, people coerced Horace by threatening to tell Narcissa on him" (*FD,* 160). To Narcissa, then, Horace transfers his feelings for his mother, and as *Sanctuary* makes clear, these emotions are strongly sexual in nature. In a dream Horace fuses the image of his mother with those of Ruby and Belle, two sexually desirable women; and then, attributing to his mother the blackness of his own forbidden thoughts, he links the imputed corruption with the evil of Popeye:

> Then he saw that she [his mother] wore a shapeless garment of faded calico and that Belle's rich, full mouth burned suddenly out of the halflight, and he knew that she was

about to open her mouth and he tried to scream at her, to clap his hand to her mouth. But it was too late. He saw her mouth open; a thick, black liquid welled in a bursting bubble that splayed out upon her fading chin and the sun was shining on his face and he was thinking He smells black. He smells like that black stuff that ran out of Bovary's mouth when they raised her head. (*SOT,* 60)

Horace associates this image of black corruption with Little Belle too, in a passage in *Sanctuary,* where he also fuses the figure of his stepdaughter with the rape of Temple Drake:

Lying with her head lifted slightly, her chin depressed like a figure lifted down from a crucifix, she watched something black and furious go roaring out of her pale body. She was bound naked on her back on a flat car moving at speed through a black tunnel, the blackness streaming in rigid threads overhead, a roar of iron wheels in her ears. The car shot bodily from the tunnel in a long upward slant, the darkness overhead now shredded with parallel attenuations of living fire, toward a crescendo like a held breath, an interval in which she would swing faintly and lazily in nothingness filled with pale, myriad points of light. Far beneath her she could hear the faint, furious uproar of the shucks. (*SOT,* 220)

Little Belle admittedly is a character who has little to recommend her, but Horace's perception of her, like his impression of his mother, appears to be colored by an imputed evil—the darkness perhaps of his own incestuous desires. This is suggested certainly by the changes that seem to occur in Little Belle's photograph, alterations that reveal an increased corruption with each viewing—like those of Oscar Wilde's portrait of Dorian Grey.[18] First, the eyes become "more secret than soft"; next, the image acquires an air of "crass brazenness"; finally, "the small face seemed to swoon in a voluptuous languor . . . leaving a soft and faded aftermath of invitation and voluptuous promise" (*SOT,* 146, 205, 220). The photograph's function as a reflector of Horace's own attitudes is suggested additionally by his observation that the image seems to be blurred, as if it lay "beneath disturbed water" (*SOT,* 146). Like Narcissus, Horace gazes at the face in the water, and he confronts there an image of himself and also, perhaps, the shadow of death.

A confusion of filial devotion and erotic desire is seen also in Narcissa, in her nostalgic memories of her father as a Gothicesque hero: "a darkly gallant shape romantic with smuggled edibles and with strong hard hands smelling always of a certain thrilling carbolic soap" (*FD,* 159). Of particular significance is the mention of the carbolic soap which, I believe, refers us directly to *Death in Venice.* In Mann's novella, the odor of carbolic acid pervades the streets and alleyways of Venice, a city in the grip of Asiatic cholera; and it is associated particularly with the grotesque guitarist in the band of mendicant musicians, from whom there emanates a strong smell of carbolic. The odor of disinfectant calls to mind not only the threat of cholera but also the sickness of Aschenbach's soul, the conquest of his will by the degrading and destructive love for Tadzio. Similarly, Narcissa's association of the carbolic soap with her father suggests a certain unhealthiness in her feelings for him. We are reminded also, at this point, that Will Benbow is the one responsible for the disruption of order in the family garden. In trying to destroy the formal beds, he achieved not the obliteration of the bulbs but only their dispersion, their blossoming henceforth in random and scattered clumps.[19] If Narcissa's relationship with her father, then, is tainted with incestuous feelings, her sexual interest in Horace, as his in her, may very well be the result of the thwarting and transference of oedipal love. As surrogates for their parents, Narcissa and Horace re-enact the romance of their elders, and time stands still.

The thwarting of the instinctual life which the relationship with Narcissa requires, however, is welcomed by Horace and accounts, in large measure, for his attraction to her; for Horace is a man who has all along attempted to deny the demands of the flesh. "Nerve-sick," "thin," and "delicate," he bears a remarkable resemblance to the frail and fastidious Aschenbach, a man who has "restrained and chilled his emotions" (*DV*, 19–20). For Horace as for Aschenbach, the restraint of the physical and the concomitant cultivation of the spiritual are represented in the imagery of the hills and the heights. These lofty regions Horace clearly associates with Narcissa; on the happy night of his homecoming, he lies on his bed and journeys to the stars:

> that wild fantastic futility of his voyaged in lonely regions of its own beyond the moon, about meadows nailed with firmamented stars to the ultimate roof of things, where unicorns filled the neighing air with galloping, or grazed or lay supine in latent and golden-hooved repose. (*FD*, 159)

Although the scene includes the unicorn, a Dionysian animal with the beard of a goat and the tail of a lion, in this vision the mythical creature poses no threat. In *Sanctuary* also, Horace associates the heights with Narcissa; again and again he tells Ruby that he came back home because he had to get away from country that was "flat and rich and foul" (and which he has identified with Belle) and because he "just had to have a hill to lie on for a while."[20]

Horace is unquestionably a man in retreat from the world. Bearing the name of a poet of classical Rome (Aschenbach is called a classical poet), Horace is the scholar and the idealist, a person most at home in the ivory tower. His stay at Oxford University was for him "a perfect life, a life accomplishing itself placidly in a region remote from time," the timelessness of this world reminiscent of Narcissa and the urn (*FD*, 163). Like Gail Hightower of *Light in August*, he sees the ministry as a haven from the turbulence of living; he covets the life of the Episcopal priest because it promises "quiet and dull peace," words associated repeatedly with his sister. It is certainly an existence without vitality and without sexuality which Horace has embraced. Trying to persuade Narcissa to remain with him instead of marrying Bayard, he tells her that sex "is not anything to give up; you don't know but I do" (*SOT*, 18). Ineffectual and impractical, Horace is a thinker and, above all, a talker, but he is not a man of action. Miss Jenny says that he "has spent so much time being educated that he never has learned anything"; and Ruby observes in *Sanctuary* that he has "the voice of a man given to talk and not much else" (*FD*, 193; *S*, 13).

Narcissa is as incomplete and fractured, psychically, as her brother, but she, like Mann's Tadzio, represents the other half of man's nature, the pole of sensation as opposed to that of spirit. She is impulsive, unreflective, and even a little dull. Horace knows that she will not understand his letter, which indeed means nothing to her; and Miss Jenny tells her, " 'You don't wonder. You just do things and then stop until the next time to do something comes around' " (*S*, 180). Closely associated with the plant and animal world, Narcissa is the embodiment of the instinctual and the unconscious. We are told that she "had never been given to talking, living a life of serene vegetation like perpetual corn or wheat in a sheltered garden instead of a field" (*S*, 103). And Horace sees in her "the supreme and stupid placidity of a cow being milked," a metaphor which may also suggest, in recalling *Paradise Lost* and Satan's comparison of the interdicted apples with "the Teats / Of Ewe or Goat dropping with Milk," that Horace regards his sister as forbidden fruit (*SOT*, 17; *PL* IX.581–82).[21] Narcissa, however, is not a sexual creature; she is the "unravished bride of quietude" (*FD*, 162). Her identification with the gods would seem to indicate, in the light of Faulkner's poetry (XLII and XXVI in *A Green Bough*), that she has not experienced the "rupture of sense and spirit" which has been man's curse since the seduction of Eve. But the Benbow Arcadia is a dying world, like that of *The Marble Faun*, which "has grown so old there is virtually no sexual activity."[22] The pole of sensation that Narcissa occupies, then, does not denote sexuality and fertility; she is able, therefore, to provide a safe harbor for Horace's affections, representing a side of his own nature he has denied while, at the same time, forbidding the exercise of those feelings he wishes to keep submerged.

Narcissa also resembles the enigmatic Tadzio, a character as paradoxical and ambivalent as she, in the role which she plays in the creative process, her function not only as a source of inspiration but also as a subject for art. The two characters are depicted often as pieces of statuary: pale, serene, and godlike; and they are also identified closely—fused almost—with the creations of Horace and Aschenbach. In fact, in the eyes of the two artists, Narcissa and Tadzio represent the very essence of art; they personify that elusive ideal of beauty which the artist pursues. They demonstrate also the perils which are inherent in the creative process, the danger that the discipline and control demanded by the art—the artist's suppression in himself of those very qualities he endeavors to capture in his work—will trigger extremes of an opposite nature. Such a possibility is pointed out in the Platonic dialogue of Aschenbach's dream:

> "But form and openness, Phaedrus, lead to intoxication and to desire, lead the noble perhaps into sinister revels of emotion which his own beautiful rigour rejects as infamous, lead to the precipice—yes, they too lead to the precipice." (*DV*, 120–21)

This warning is conveyed also in *Flags in the Dust*: the Venetian cave where the glass-blowers work is depicted as an inferno; Horace's workshop—"a cave," "a dungeon," "a furnace"—carries in its description echoes of Milton's Hell. What is required, actually, by truly great art is a blending of discipline and freedom, form and feeling—a balance which is difficult to achieve and impossible to maintain. Only once in his life does Aschenbach reach this zenith, that time when, inspired by the beauty of Tadzio, he composes the essay that elicits the wonder and admiration of his readers; it is a work that is produced, we are told, by the "rare creative intercourse between the spirit and body" (*DV*, 81). At times Horace, too, manages to weld discipline with feeling, those occasions when the road becomes sunlit again, and he carries to Narcissa his nearly-perfect vases, "his face blackened too with smoke and a little mad, passionate and fine and austere" (*FD*, 194).[23]

As the two opposing poles of the psyche, Horace and Narcissa, like Aschenbach and Tadzio, can be regarded as the complementary halves of a single personality; their relationship, then, becomes an exercise in self-love, in which each of the partners is drawn to the reflection of himself he sees in the other. Narcissism is in fact a primary ingredient in the incestuous relationship, as Milton also demonstrates in *Paradise Lost*; there Sin reminds Satan of the source of his attraction to her: "Thyself in me thy perfect image viewing / Becam'st enamor'd" (*PL* II.765–66). And quite appropriately, we find clumps of narcissus (and its cousin the jonquil) growing haphazardly in the Benbow garden. Narcissa, pointedly, bears the name of the mythical youth who fell in love with his reflection and pined away and died; Narcissus-like, she is associated with a multitude of reflecting devices: glass doors, mirrors, pools of water, and windows. In *Death in Venice*, also, doubling is suggested by the repeated and insistent use of reflecting devices: Tadzio walks through glass doors; his smile is likened to Narcissus' over the mirroring pool; Aschenbach gazes at himself in the mirror or the glass; he drinks pomegranate juice from a glass, and he studies the hourglass. Additionally, Horace's and Aschenbach's identification of Narcissa and Tadzio with their works of art signifies a reflection of sorts and points also to the narcissism inherent in the creative process. Horace gives Narcissa's name to his blown-glass vase; Aschenbach sees Tadzio as the mirror of his art, and he feels at times a father's love for the boy, the affection of the creator of beauty for its possessor. As the attitudes of Aschenbach and Horace suggest, the artist's love for his art, the creation of his mind just as surely as the child is the product of the flesh, is at heart an incestuous one.

Such relationships are innately disastrous.[24] In *Flags in the Dust*, this ruin is predicted in the description of the Benbow garden: the flowers bloom in "random clumps"; the "cinderpacked drive" rises in "a grave curve"; dark cedars exude a "resinous exhilarating gloom"; the house itself bears a "funereal Tudor" design. Narcissa is linked so often with images of doom as to be considered a figure of death. She is drawn strangely to the parlor of the Sartoris house, a room that is associated with death and one which Aunt Jenny, a strong and positive person who stands for the continuation of the family, dislikes and refuses to use. She is identified often with the image of the Grecian urn, which represents stasis, the antithesis of motion and life. Her depiction as the "unravished bride" places her in a dying world, one in which sexuality has virtually disappeared. She appears most persistently, however, in the metaphor of still water.[25] She is likened to "the windless surface of a pool" and a "tideless summer sea" in which Horace's spirit drowses—images as void of life and motion as those of the frozen figures on Keat's Grecian urn (*FD*, 160, 161). Pools of water in *Flags in the Dust* function also as mirrors, and both images are fused often with Narcissa, and both point to death. As a youth, Old Bayard looks into the spring and sees reflected there an image of his own mortality; in the mirror beside the parlor's folding doors, the glass "filled with grave obscurity like a still pool of evening water," Narcissa makes the same discovery (*FD*, 10).

Tadzio too is identified with water; the most striking images in *Death in Venice* are those of Tadzio at the beach—poised against the shoreline, entering the sea, or emerging from it. He is in fact defined by the sea that serves so often as his backdrop; its qualities are his own. Unfortunately, it is precisely those qualities in Tadzio that account for Aschenbach's obsession with the boy:

He loved the ocean for deep-seated reasons: because of that yearning for rest, when the hard-pressed artist hungers to shut out the exacting multiplicities of experience and hide himself on the breast of the simple, the vast; and because of a forbidden hankering—seductive, by virtue of its being directly opposed to his obligations—after the incommunicable, the incommensurate, the eternal, the non-existent. To be at rest in the face of perfection is the hunger of everyone who is aiming at excellence; and what is the non-existent but a form of perfection? But now, just as his dreams were so far out in vacancy, suddenly the horizontal fringe of the sea was broken by a human figure. . . . (*DV, 56*)

Nothingness, perfection, rest, the simple, the eternal, the incommunicable and incommensurate: these words also describe Narcissa. The full significance of the water imagery, however, is made clear in *Death in Venice,* where the dying Aschenbach imagines that Tadzio calls him from the shore and that he follows his summoner into the sea.

In Faulkner's novel, the implications of the water imagery are most evident, perhaps, in the Benbows' rainy-day reunion in the book's fourth section. Focusing insistently on wetness and water, the scene stresses Narcissa's attempts to bring Horace in from the rain that has motion and life, unlike the still water associated with her, and to prevent, metaphorically, the entrance of her brother into the world.[26] At the same time, though, the pair's wet embrace and the taste of rain in their kiss reveal the hidden passions of their own relationship, a development that promises, in their case however, not life but disaster. Here, as in Maugham's "Rain," another story about the revenge of repressed desire, the rain seems to symbolize "the malignancy of the primitive powers of nature."[27] It conveys the same meaning, also, in *The Sound and the Fury,* where it pervades Quentin's doomed and despairing recollections of his and Caddy's lusts. In the Compson's story and in "Rain," however, the ruin predicted in *Flags in the Dust* is fully accomplished with the suicides of Quentin and the Reverend Davidson.

The seeds of destruction which have lain buried in the Benbow garden do eventually take root and bloom but not in Horace's and Narcissa's relationship; instead they flourish in the Benbows' relationships with other characters, who represent aspects of Horace's and Narcissa's thwarted natures. It is a device easily recognized in *Death in Venice,* where the supporting characters also serve to comment on the story's protagonist. In the novella, there appear periodically certain figures who are distinguished by similar or identical features: slightness of build, a fair complexion, a snub-nose, curling lips or licking tongues, furrowed brow, grinning mouth, red hair, a red tie, a straw hat. Conveying, in their identification with one another, the impression of one recurrent figure, of a leitmotif of sorts, these characters are fused also with Tadzio and Aschenbach and, together with Tadzio, represent certain aspects of Aschenbach's nature: those repressed instincts which eventually destroy him.

One of the doomed affairs that serves as surrogate for the Benbows' forbidden love is the tawdry courtship (and the disastrous marriage) of Horace and Belle. Its function is suggested primarily by Horace's identification of Narcissa with Belle, whom he regards also as stupid and whom he sees too in the metaphor of the sea—an ocean "in which he watched himself drown" (*FD*, 243). The tendency to link the two women is revealed most explicitly, however, in the original *Sanctuary*:

> He tried to think of his sister, of Belle. But they seemed interchangeable now: two tiny, not distinguishable figures like two china figurines seen backward through a telescope. (*SOT*, 27)

This confusion enables Horace, imaginatively at least, to consummate his love for Narcissa in the seduction of Belle. The function of Horace's relationship with Belle, its use as a vehicle for the instincts' revenge, is indicated in his attempt to explain to Narcissa his attraction to Belle:

> "That may be the secret, after all. Not any subconscious striving after what we believed will be happines, contentment; but a sort of gadfly urge after the petty, ignoble impulses which man has tried so vainly to conjure with words out of himself. Nature, perhaps, watching him as he tries to wean himself away from the rank and richly foul old mire that spawned him, biding her time and flouting that illusion of purifaction which he has foisted upon himself and calls his soul." (*FD*, 288–89)

That this is the case is supported, of course, by the blatant sexuality of Belle's appeal. Like Mann's vulgar and lascivious guitarist and the threatening man at the mortuary portals, she has red hair—"a rich bloody auburn"; and she is described as a tiger and "a great still cat," images that summon Aschenbach's torrid jungle.[28]

Like her sister Belle, whom she resembles in her flaming hair and her feline nature, Joan Heppleton provides Horace also with an outlet for his feeling for Narcissa. Her portrait, however, is painted in stronger and harsher colors and reveals a sensuality that is even more pronounced. Horace's response to Joan, moreover, contains the same ambivalence as his attitude toward Belle; he is powerfully attracted and at the same time frightened and repulsed. Narcissa also experiences these paradoxical emotions in her courtship with Bayard, whom Joan in fact resembles in many ways. Like him, she is savage and brutal, violent and threatening, but also forthright and honest, "tragic and austere and fine."

The Benbows' relationship is elucidated, additionally, by Byron Snopes's infatuation with Narcissa. A character who provides the book's most extreme example of repression and license, Snopes is identified in many ways with the Benbows. Like Horace, he is defeated in his pursuit of Narcissa by the "impotence" of his desire. With Narcissa he shares a penchant for deviousness and a fondness for the forbidden. The sly secretive Snopes with his covert eyes, inflectionless voice, and soundless movements is in fact cut from the same cloth as Narcissa, who does not like Shakespeare because he has no secrets, who hides Byron's letters to read later in secret, who could not be shocked by his last obscene letter even if she'd understood. Like both the Benbows, he is associated with images of confinement and entrapment; his grilled teller's cage in Colonel Sartoris' bank is an apt metaphor for his state. All three, also, are linked to Lord Byron. Snopes bears his name, and his portrait parodies that of a Byronic hero. Horace and Narcissa employ Byron's phrases to frame their thoughts (echoes of *Don Juan* appear in Horace's letter to his sister and in one of Narcissa's conversations with Aunt Jenny), and their incestuous love recalls that of Lord Byron and his half-sister, Augusta. Snopes resembles the Benbows also in his efforts at sublimation—his attempts to release the thwarted passion for Narcissa in the fumblings and gropings with Minnie Sue. The parallels do not, of course, bode well for the Benbows. When Byron, on his last furtive visit to the Benbow house, crashes through the window into "a shallow, glassed flower pit," he concludes his pursuit of Narcissa with a symbolic and a Miltonic fall into Hell (*FD*, 256).

The one character who is juxtaposed most persistently to Horace and Narcissa is Bayard Sartoris. Sometimes he serves as a foil; he is a man of action in contrast to Horace, a man of thought (like Bayard's poetical brother). In many ways, though, Bayard is identified with the Benbows: he too is a victim of self-imposed walls, and he also suffers a terrible disunion in his nature. Following the accident on the stallion, both he and Narcissa experience this schism in the psyche, the old opposition of the mind and body, the heart and head: Bayard lies in Buck's bed in the jailkeeper's quarters, and "it was as though his head were one Bayard who watched curiously and impersonally that other Bayard who lay in a strange bed"; Narcissa lies in bed with a book and holds "her consciousness deliberately submerged as you hold a puppy under water until its body ceases to resist" (*FD*, 143, 138). These tendencies, which have been present in Narcissa from the beginning, are of course exacerbated by the attraction to Bayard which leaves her fearful yet fascinated, repelled and drawn. The split in the psyche is represented, moreover, in both Bayard's and Horace's imaginations by the flight to the heavens, an association that recalls Aschenbach's identification of the mountain peaks with the discipline—the "coldly passionate service"—required by his art (*DV*, 19). The celestial journey represents for Bayard, however, not the repression of love but its irreparable loss; for Horace the peaks signify the sister he cannot have, for Bayard the brother he has lost. But in Bayard's case, as in Horace's, the anguish he suffers—the repression and consequent explosion of his emotions, the division of his nature, and his sense of incompleteness—derives from the disruption of the sibling relationship. That the very closeness of the Sartoris twins made inevitable the tragedy of their lives is a possibility suggested in an early photograph of the boys: "They were not long definitely out of babyhood, yet there was already upon the infantile chubbiness of their faces a shadow as though from the propinquity of the faces above them" (*SOT*, 42). The tragedy lies in the fact that the earlier closeness cannot be maintained, nor once lost, can it ever be recovered. In either case, Benbow or Sartoris, the sibling relationship is itself a metaphor for man's incompleteness; twinning points to the fall from wholeness and incest to the strain to regain it.[29]

In *Mosquitoes* the two relationships are fused in the incestuous love of the Robyn twins.[30] Pat Robyn's unusually strong attachment to her brother Josh is evident early in the book in her jealousy of Jenny and in her insistence on following Josh to Yale, but it is not until the final chapter that the note of perversion really enters the relationship. The last night of their stay in New Orleans, Pat persuades Josh to let her enter his bed and then to allow her to indulge in what was evidently a customary practice: to take his ear "between her teeth, biting it just a little, making a kind of meaningless maternal sound against his ear" (*M*, 317). This ratlike nibbling of the ear anticipates the appearance of the lascivious rats in the novel's closing pages, where, "keen and plump as death," they "steal out to gnaw" the beggar's crust of bread and to sniff obscenely at "his intimate parts" (*M*, 336). Their eyes glowing like cigarettes, the hot-bellied rats seem to represent here, as they do in other Faulkner works, unbridled appetite or a perverted lust.[31] The mouth at the ear also suggests Milton's Satan, in the shape of a toad, whispering in the ear of the sleeping Eve; this act, which prefaces the Fall, seems to plant in her the seeds of corruption and to render her susceptible to the serpent's assault.[32] Similarly, the mouth at the ear in *Mosquitoes* promises to be the precursor of some more serious event. In *Mosquitoes*, as in *Flags in the Dust*, this incestuous behavior is related to a sense of incompleteness and loss. After she returns to her room, Pat lies naked in her bed and dreams of finding herself on "a high place," in much the same way that Horace, after a conversation with Narcissa, journeys to the heights or that Bayard, in despair at the death of his twin, travels to the "black and savage stars." An earlier unity or wholeness is suggested certainly in the blurring of gender in each of the twins and the answering of both to the name of

Gus, phenomena which imply a reduplication in one person of the other or the division of some prior androgynous being. In this case, too, the incest seems to signify a straining toward an earlier wholeness, an effort to repair the division that the twinning represents.

In *Flags in the Dust,* the equation of the two sibling relationships, a balancing of structural elements that stresses the imbalance in the souls of the characters, is implied particularly in the scene of Bayard's fatal crash. This identification is achieved primarily by the use of linking imagery, the employment in the description of the biplane's crack-up in Daytona of images which are taken from scenes in Horace's and Narcissa's lives: the speed of the dive alone keeps the plane "from falling like an inside out *umbrella*"; the tail of the plane swings "in a soaring *arc*"; the "*wing*tips" buckle and then the wings fall off [italics mine] (*FD*, 357–58). Of particular significance is the image of the wings, which brings to mind the "fallen" wings of Narcissa's hair and recalls especially Bayard's perception of them as the "twin dark wings of hair" (*FD*, 122). In the use of this phrase in his hellish hallucination after his fall from the horse, Bayard fuses the image of Narcissa with that of John and the anguish of his life without his twin. The identification is a telling one. Bayard hopes to find in Narcissa the release he has sought since the death of John, but it is a release not from grief but from life; for the peace that Narcissa represents is synonymous with death.[33]

In one of the novel's last scenes, Miss Jenny's visit to the Jefferson cemetery, this use of imagery as a linking device is even more pronounced. The images used in the description of the Sartoris gravesites are those which have appeared previously in the Benbow sections: "marble shapes," "impervious stone," "peaceful simplicity," "symbolical urns," "clipped tended sward," "black cedars," "random bursts" of flowers, "withered flowers," "carven eyes," "carven gestures" (*FD*, 363–66). One phrase in particular binds together the Benbow and Sartoris halves of the book: "their arrogant lusts." It is a phrase which points to the Fall; in the arrogance of the Sartorises is found its cause, and in the lusts of the Benbows its immediate result.[34]

The two families actually converge in the child Benbow Sartoris, who appropriately bears the names of both; and in his personal destiny rests the fate of both clans. The signs, however, do not augur well for the survival of either. In the tableau of the novel's conclusion, where Miss Jenny and Narcissa are pictured in the parlor at twilight, the imagery points again to stasis and death: "Beyond Miss Jenny's trim fading head the window curtains hung motionless without any wind; beyond the window evening was a windless lilac dream, foster-dam of quietude and peace" (*FD*, 370).[35] Benbow's appearances in two other works of this period also offer little promise of a felicitous ending. His physical resemblance to Bayard which is noted in *Sanctuary*—the same back, the sullen mouth, the bleak and brooding eyes—implies that Benbow will follow in his father's footsteps, that he too will re-enact the Sartoris legend; Narcissa's domination of Benbow in "There was a Queen"—her insistence that he abandon his place at the head of the table for a chair beside her—hints that she will guide "Bory" into the role played earlier by brother "Hory." Regardless of the path that he chooses, the arrogant pride of the Sartorises or the incestuous love of the Benbows, the heir apparent appears to be doomed.[36]

Incest in *Flags in the Dust*, then, occurs primarily in the Benbow sections of the book and focuses principally on the relationship of Narcissa and Horace, although it does include other relationships as well: Horace and his mother, Horace and Little Belle, Narcissa and her father. A metaphor of the fall from wholeness, incest in this novel points to the duality of man, a theme which appears to owe much to Thomas Mann and his novella *Death in Venice*. Like Mann, Faulkner is concerned with man's inability to bring into some sort of harmonious relationship the two halves of his being. In this schism of the psyche, sense opposes spirit, and the body, the mind; thought represses feeling, and the emotions exact their revenge. In both Faulkner's work and Mann's, this contest is dramatized in the divided souls of the stories' characters, in their representation as one or the other of the self's opposing halves; in general, the protagonists depict the spiritual part of man, while those emotions which they have denied are reflected and revealed in the books' lesser figures. In both of the stories, the fall from wholeness leads to ruin, a devastation that is adumbrated in the garden imagery of a fallen world.

3

The Sound and the Fury

The concept of the Fall is central also to *The Sound and the Fury,* a novel
which was written two years later than *Flags in the Dust* but which followed *Sartoris* into print by a matter of nine months. The book's inception, according to Faulkner, lay in a "mental picture," the image of "the
muddy seat of a little girl's drawers in a pear tree where she could see
through a window where her grandmother's funeral was taking place and
report what was happening to her brothers on the ground below."[1] The
symbolic content of the picture is clear: it is the depiction of innocence
soiled, acquiring knowledge of evil and looking on death. The strength
with which this image gripped Faulkner's imagination is revealed in his
introduction to the novel, written in 1933, where he characterized this
picture of Caddy in the tree as "perhaps the only thing in literature which
would ever move me very much."[2] Faulkner maintained, moreover, that
the entire novel grew out of repeated efforts to explain this one image,
that each section in the book represented yet another attempt to tell "that
same story."[3] The story which he sought to tell is "the tragedy of two
lost women: Caddy and her daughter."[4] It is also, however, a chronicle
of the ruin of the Compsons and suggests, as well, the fall of the South.

Ultimately, however, it is the story of the Fall of man. At issue is the
age-old problem of the existence of evil in the world; Faulkner makes this
clear when he states that "Quentin was still trying to get God to tell him
why, in *Absalom, Absalom!* as he was in *The Sound and the Fury.*"[5] The
answer which Faulkner provides is one with Milton's in his effort to "justify the ways of God to men": man himself is to blame for the suffering
in the world (*PL*, I.26). In order to persuade man to recognize his culp-
ability and to assume the burden of this responsibility, Faulkner like Milton feels it necessary first to impress upon him the ugliness of evil; and
Faulkner too finds in incest the best metaphor for the horror of sin.

The concepts, then, which concern Faulkner in *The Sound and the
Fury* remain much the same as in *Flags in the Dust.* The structure of this
novel, however, departs radically from that of the earlier work; in *The*

Sound and the Fury Faulkner reveals for the first time his fascination with the fragmentation of truth and men's widely diverging perceptions of reality, an interest which is evidenced in his use of four separate sections and four different perspectives to tell one story. Much has been made of the novel's narrative technique by the critics, who have advanced a variety of theories as to what the divisions represent: Freudian personality components, parallels of Christ, aspects of innocence, types of apprehension, symphonic movements, two objective narrations framing two subjective ones, and the movement from a private to a public world.[6] Cleanth Brooks has viewed the four sections "under the rubric of poetry," in relation to time, and according to conceptions of love.[7]

Another way of regarding the structure of the novel is to examine the sections in the light of Milton's faculty psychology, a concept which is presented in one of *Paradise Lost*'s best known passages. Here Raphael employs the analogy of the tree—an image which is central to both *Paradise Lost* and *The Sound and the Fury*—to demonstrate to Adam the order which exists in nature and in man's soul:

> So from the root
> Springs lighter the green stalk, from thence the leaves
> More aery, last the bright consummate flow'r
> Spirits odorous breathes: flow'rs and thir fruit
> Man's nourishment, by gradual scale sublim'd
> To vital spirits aspire, to animal,
> To intellectual, give both life and sense,
> Fancy and understanding, whence the Soul
> Reason receives, and reason is her being. . . .
> (*PL* V.479–87)

This passage, certainly, is one which was familiar to Faulkner; it is paraphrased twice in *The Hamlet,* in passages which frame the lyrical description of Ike's love affair with the cow. As Ike watches the coming of the new day, he observes the light, not descending from the sky but rising instead out of the ground:

> it wakes, upseeping, attritive in uncountable creeping: first, root; then frond by frond, from whose escaping tips like gas it rises and disseminates and stains the sleep-fast earth with drowsy insect-murmur. . . .

In the evening the process is reversed:

> Then ebb's afternoon, until at last the morning, noon and afternoon flow back, drain the sky and creep leaf by voiceless leaf and twig and branch and trunk, descending, gathering frond by frond among the grass, still creeping down in drowsy insect murmurs.[8]

Milton's narrator, Raphael, is also important to Faulkner. The name appears in *As I Lay Dying,* where Rafe MacCallum's twin, like Raphael in *Paradise Lost,* serves as a herald of harm, warning the Bundrens that the flood has washed out the bridge; the significance of the name is stressed in this passage by the narrator's inability to recall the name of Rafe's twin, a device to draw attention to the name not of the twin but of Rafe himself. And in *Flags in the Dust* we meet Rafe (Raphael Semmes) MacCallum, a man of "easy manner" and "loquacious," like Milton's angel—a spirit "gentle," "sociable," "affable," and "mild" (*FD,* 310, 325; *PL* V.221, VII.41, VIII.648, XI.23).

In *Paradise Lost* these various faculties—sense, fancy, and reason—are perhaps best explained in a conversation which Adam holds with Eve; here he points out the function of each faculty and notes its place in the hierarchy of man's soul:

> But know that in the Soul
> Are many lesser faculties that serve
> Reason as chief; among these Fancy next
> Her office holds, of all external things,
> Which the five watchful Senses represent,
> She forms Imagination, Aery shapes,
> Which Reason joining or disjoining, frames
> All what we affirm or what deny, and call
> Our knowledge or opinion; then retires
> Into her private Cell when Nature rests.
> Oft in her absence mimic Fancy wakes
> To imitate her; but misjoining shapes,
> Wild work produces oft, and most in dreams,
> Ill matching words and deeds long past or late.
> (*PL* V.100–113)

In *The Sound and the Fury,* then, each of these faculties is represented by one of the Compson brothers: Benjy typifies the senses; Quentin, fancy and imagination; and Jason, reason—albeit reason gone astray. The three brothers, in a sense, merge to form one composite man, a kind of Compson Adam.[9] Each brother is identified with the other two just as their monologues—replete with similar or identical images, gestures, and phrases—mirror one another. One of the most significant ways in which the brothers resemble one another is in their obsession with their sister or her surrogate Quentin, in the incestuous feelings each harbors for Caddy or her daughter.

Benjy is a person who operates entirely at the level of the senses. He cannot think; he can only feel, "like something eyeless and voiceless which might have lived, existed merely because of its ability to suffer, in the beginning of life. . . ."[10] He is in fact little more than an animal. The embodiment of sense sundered from spirit, he illustrates perfectly the splintering of man as a result of the Fall.

With his cornflower blue eyes and his childlike innocence, Benjy emerges as a kind of prelapsarian Adam, a condition that in Faulkner, however, is far from desirable. Innocence is often associated with villains, such as Sutpen and Popeye, who do not recognize evil for what it is, or with men like Hightower and Ike McCaslin, who fail to come to grips with the world and assume their share of life's burdens. It is a quality which is dangerous, if not to others, at least to oneself. It assuredly does not denote the pure goodness of sinless man, as we see also in the story of Ike Snopes of *The Hamlet,* an innocent that Benjy anticipates in many ways and one who is depicted more clearly as one of the "fallen and unregenerate Seraphim" (*H,* 183).[11] Ike's corrupted nature is suggested certainly in the Miltonic echoes in the interlude with the cow.[12] Like Adam, who makes for Eve a wreath that sheds its faded roses at her Fall, Ike fashions for his love a garland of flowers which wilt and scatter before they can crown the beloved's head; like Eve, who becomes enamoured of her own reflection in the pool, Ike and the cow drink from the spring, "each face to its own shattered image wedded and annealed" (*H,* 183). The two passages which frame this pastoral scene are indebted to Raphael's analogy of the tree, a figure which is employed to illustrate the lesson that all life derives from and returns to God. In *The Hamlet,* however, the movement is reversed: as the day dawns, the light rises from earth to sky; and in the evening, it returns to the earth. Clearly, the divine order of which Raphael speaks is not to be found here, in either nature or man. Ike remains, like Benjy, one of the unnamed and homeless angels.

Despite his innocence, then, Benjy is fallen man, and it is most assuredly a blighted garden where he dwells. In the Compson enclosure, the ground is "hard, churned, and knotted" and the flowers "rasped and rattled." His "graveyard" there is adorned with fennel, a favorite food of the serpent in *Paradise Lost;* adjacent to this Eden lies a pen of "grunting and snuffing pigs," animals associated in the novel with sex and death.[13] Such a world provides no redemption, no promise of human warmth or love, a point that is made in the novel's first paragraph, where Benjy follows the progress of a golf game in what was formerly his pasture. The items depicted here—flowers, flags, table (or altar), tree (or cross), fence (or rail)—denote the objects of the sanctuary and provide a eucharistic setting; but hitting takes place within, and Benjy remains fenced out. The sense of isolation which pervades Benjy's section is conveyed also in the image of the door, which Benjy likens to mirrors or to the dark places on the wall. They do not provide passages to other people, to warmth and understanding; they are blank spaces, dark unlit areas, or reflectors.

The one scene, however, that dominates Benjy's narrative and which points most vividly to a Miltonic Fall is that of Caddy in her muddy drawers climbing the pear tree to look in the window at her grandmother's funeral. This image describes, of course, the Fall of Eve, the rebel yielding to temptation and acquiring knowledge of sex and death. The scene's fidelity to Milton's version of the myth is evident in a remarkable number of details: Caddy's ignorance of her grandmother's death, her denial of it when she is told, Mr. Compson's injunctions against climbing the tree, Caddy's rationalizations for acting in defiance of her father, and finally the willful disobedience itself. The image here of the muddy drawers anticipates, of course, Caddy's eventual corruption, her surrender to the heat of passion that is clearly linked, in Benjy's memories of an older and more experienced sister, to the lust of Eve; his recollections of the "little points of fire . . . in her eyes" and "the eyes that flew at him" recall Eve, "whose Eye darted contagious Fire" in response to Adam's appetite for sex after the fruit has been eaten (*SF,* 84, 88; *PL* IX.1034). In this scene, Caddy is identified with the serpent, again like Eve, who is linked to the snake, particularly in Adam's rejection of her after the Fall, in his epithet: "thou, Serpent" (*PL* X.867). Just as the serpent, at least in his account to Eve, climbs the tree of knowledge while the other animals "with like desire / Longing and envying stood," so Caddy shinnies up the pear tree as the less daring brothers cluster around and watch (*PL* IX.589–93). It is no accident that the clear-eyed Dilsey, undeceived by disguises here as always, should fix upon Caddy the name of "Satan." It is a judgment with which we concur, reluctantly however; for Caddy wins our hearts. The ambivalence that is perceived in Caddy's character is but further evidence, though, of her kinship with Satan. Like him, she is strong, courageous, and determined, providing us in part with a model to emulate; but she too has charted her course in the wrong direction, demonstrating what it is that we must vigorously oppose.

The Fall is also indicated in Benjy's section by his affection for Caddy, a love which goes beyond the bounds of familial feeling. His desire for his sister is best revealed in the abortive attack upon the Burgess girl, an assault which "must be viewed as an attempt at incest" inasmuch as the girl "functions as a substitute for Caddy."[14] His association of this girl with Caddy is clearly indicated in the location where the attack takes place: the gate where he had customarily awaited his sister's return from school and where he still goes to look for her. Benjy's action, however, is not an intentional act of violence but rather a desperate effort to communicate, almost an involuntary act. In the manner of Melville's Billy

Budd, who strikes Claggart when his stutter renders him mute, the speechless Benjy avails himself of the only recourse that he sees open to him—a physical contact. Benjy's relationship with Caddy also acquires sexual overtones through the imagery of the golf game; the words "caddy" and "balls" link his sister with his gelding and remind us that castration has been the traditional punishment for incest.[15]

The theme of incest is suggested, additionally, by the enigmatic passage on the "bluegum" and its oblique reference to Freud's Myth of the Primal Horde. Benjy recalls here a conversation with Versh:

> *Versh said, Your name Benjamin now. You know how come your name Benjamin now. They making a bluegum out of you. Mammy say in old time your grandpa changed nigger's name, and he turn preacher, and when they look at him, he turn bluegum too. Didn't use to be bluegum, neither. And when family woman look him in the eye in the full of the moon, chile born bluegum. And one evening, when they was about a dozen them bluegum chillen running around the place, he never come home. Possum hunters found him in the woods, et clean. And you know who et him. Them bluegum chillen did.* (SF, 84–85)

In the Myth of the Primal Horde, a story of rebellion and patricide in the primordial family, Freud offers his explanation for the origin of the incest taboo:

> One day the expelled brothers joined forces, slew and ate the father, and thus put an end to the father horde. Together they dared and accomplished what would have remained impossible for them singly. . . . This violent primal father had surely been the envied and feared model for each of the brothers. Now they accomplished their identification with him by devouring him and each acquired a part of his strength. The totem feast . . . would be the repetition and commemoration of this memorable, criminal act with which so many things began, social organization, moral restrictions, and religion. . . . The group of brothers banded together were dominated by . . . contradictory feelings towards the father. . . . They hated the father who stood so powerfully in the way of their sexual demands and their desire for power, but they also loved and admired him. After they had satisfied their hate . . . the suppressed tender impulses had to assert themselves. This took place in the form of remorse, a sense of guilt was formed. . . . What the father's presence had formerly prevented they themselves now prohibited. . . . They undid their deed by declaring that the killing of the father substitute, the totem, was not allowed, and renounced the fruits of their deed by denying themselves the liberated woman. . . . Whoever disobeyed became guilty of the two only crimes which troubled primitive society.[16]

Versh's story resembles Freud's in a number of significant ways: the rebellion of the sons, the fear of acting alone, the murder of the father, the cannibalistic meal. But in the point it tries to make, Versh's story represents an inversion of the Freudian myth. Although, in Versh's version, the crime is present, the remedy is not; the two taboos—the prohibitions against patricide and incest—are not instituted, and man is not ushered into a new morality. Instead, Benjy and "the nigger" lapse back into a primitive state. They are turned into "bluegums"—persons that, according to the Southern idiom, are ignorant and backward, uncivilized even.[17] In the changing of their names, and the subsequent loss of identity and birthright, they lose their footing in any sort of ordered existence. Versh's identification of Benjy as a totemic figure is supported in the book by the association of Benjy with Christ and also by the linking of him with the pig and the bear, both of which *The Golden Bough* includes in its list of totem animals. The use of passages on Caddy's moral fall to frame Versh's tale suggests the family's sacrifice of this Compson too and also, perhaps, Caddy's own part in the abandonment of Benjy.

In *As I Lay Dying,* published a year after *The Sound and the Fury* and concerned also with incest, the totem appears again. In this novel, Vardaman Bundren fuses the image of his dying mother with that of a dead fish and then envisions a sort of totem meal in which the mother is consumed and transformed: "And it [the fish] will be cooked and et and she will be him and pa and Cash and Dewey Dell and there wont be anything in the box so she can breathe."[18] In this instance, however, the effects of the ceremony appear to be mixed. As in *The Sound and the Fury,* the incest ban is not instituted, and a new morality is not ushered in. Although the more resilient Bundrens do continue, unlike the Compsons, their survival commands a high price: the loss of the Quentin-like Darl, their most sensitive member.

Suggestions of incest in Benjy's section are found also in Caddy's assumption of the role of surrogate mother, a part which seems to indicate that she, like Narcissa, is the recipient of thwarted oedipal love. Caddy feeds Benjy his meals, lies beside him in the bed to help him go to sleep, comforts him when he cries, and worries that his hands will "be froze." And she mothers Mrs. Compson as well, drying her tears and sending her upstairs where she "can be sick." Such a role reversal is not unusual in the incestuous family, clinical studies reveal, nor, interestingly, are two other components of the Compson household: the alcoholic father and the promiscuous daughter.[19]

The theme of incest is also suggested in the affliction of the youngest Compson son. A man who remained three years old for thirty years, Benjy is emblematic of the stagnation and regression, the failure to grow, that characterizes the incestuous family.[20] His restriction to the Compson grounds and his complete dependence on the family, which his condition necessitates, imply an inwardness that is often associated with incest.[21] It is a quality that describes not only Benjy and the Compsons but the South as well—a region that, since the 1830's, had closed its ranks against any kind of external influence. In addition, Benjy's shattered mind recalls the age-old biological argument against incest, the belief that the offspring of an incestuous union would be defective.[22] This is not to say that Benjy is the result of incest, for he is not. We are reminded rather that the association of these two themes—incest and idiocy—has been widespread and of long duration, that in *The Sound and the Fury* the two themes do meet in the person of Benjy, and that here they denote the same end: the demise of the Compsons.

The narrator of the second section in the novel, Quentin Compson, also represents one of the faculties in Milton's faculty psychology. He is fancy—a fancy gone awry, escaped from the government of right reason. One significant indication of the errancy of this fancy is Quentin's conviction that he has committed incest with Caddy, an offense that is no less dangerous and complex for being imagined. Its causes in fact run deep; the ramifications are many; and the results are deadly.

At the heart of Quentin's incestuous feelings is his narcissistic love of self. He is attracted to Caddy in large part because he sees her as a reflection of himself, an attitude that is revealed primarily in his association of Caddy with the image of the door. The sign of his shadow driven "into the door" reminds Quentin of Caddy's reflection in the mirror; repeatedly—no fewer than six times—Caddy is pictured "in the door." When Quentin, then, regards Caddy framed in the door, he really sees an image of himself. This use of the door as a reflecting device recalls a similar employment in *Soldier's Pay* to denote the inhibiting influences of narcissism: in pursuit of Cecily, Januarius Jones halts at a closed door and confronts "in its polished depths the fat white blur of his own face," "the bulky tweeded Narcissus of himself in the polished wood" (*SP*, 91, 92). But this kind of self-communication is what Quentin desires. As he notes in his comments on Benjy and the mirror, it is the sameness of the reflection—the absence of otherness—which is responsible for its charm: "How we used to sit before that mirror. Refuge unfailing in which conflict tempered silenced reconciled" (*SF*, 211). What Quentin seeks in his relationship with Caddy is a refuge from "the multiplicity of conflicts of opposites," which, according to Andrew Lytle, characterizes life in the fallen world. Incest, Lytle tells us, is the symbol for "an habitual impulse, the refusal to engage in the cooperating opposites that make life"; the brother and sister withdraw from the stresses of the outside world and resort to one another "in an effort to return to the prenatural equilibrium of innocence and wholeness."[23]

Another reflecting device appears in the form of Shreve's glasses. Sometimes these glasses, "glinting . . . like little pools," seem to indicate Quentin's identification with Shreve, but more often they point to the fusing of Shreve with Caddy. The description of Caddy running out of the mirror and out of the scent of roses is followed by a reference to Shreve's glasses, which "glinted rosily"; the comparison of Shreve's glasses to "small yellow moons" recalls Mr. Compson's reference, in a conversation about Caddy, to woman's "periodic filth between two moons balanced" (*SF*, 95, 159, 208). A similar blending of identities occurs in the triad of Quentin, Caddy, and Ames, in which the two sparring men regard one another through the piece of colored glass which is Caddy. In both of these triangular relationships, the third man—Shreve and Ames—seems to act as a vehicle for the incest in a way that anticipates "the pure and perfect incest" of yet another threesome: Judith, Henry, and Bon of *Absalom, Absalom!*

Another cause for Quentin's attraction to incest is pride, a characteristic, like narcissism, of the original sin. Like Satan and Eve in *Paradise Lost*, Quentin wants to arrogate to himself the prerogatives of God, an overreaching that is best expressed in the Appendix's description of him:

> who loved not the idea of the incest which he would not commit, but some presbyterian concept of its eternal punishment: he, not God, could by that means cast himself and his sister both into hell, where he could guard her forever and keep her forevermore intact amid the eternal fires.[24]

As Robert Jacobs points out, "It is hard to construe this comment as other than an assessment of pride. For all of Quentin Compson's gentleness, his love of the idiot Benjy, his agonizing over injustice, he is unwilling to leave God's business to God."[25] Such an interpretation finds added support in the Appendix's statement that Quentin flings himself into the death that he longs for as a mistress because he "can no longer bear not the refraining but the restraint" (*SFA*, 411). The use here of "restraint" recalls Milton's "one restraint," God's injunction against the eating of the indicted fruit; and it points to Quentin's defiance, his attraction not to the incest (just as Eve is not really tempted by the fruit) but to the forbidden, the revolt. The arrogance of incest is, perhaps, best explained by Elliott Coleman in a discussion which Jacobs draws to our attention:

> It represents a desire for self-sufficiency. . . . What a great temptation, how god-like, to be whole, to be alone, unified, integral, to be the more completely self-sufficient, entirely independent, something reserved for a deity, by union with a part of oneself. And I would add, doomed to fail, because a totally new thing, another and new wholeness, a further reach, is not thereby arrived at in a unique creative act, but rather, a retrogression to solipsism. . . .[26]

This desire for banishment, described in the Appendix, Quentin voices earlier in the text, in the confused recollections which have been triggered by the ringing of the Harvard chimes:

> Because if it were just to hell; if that were all of it. Finished. If things just finished themselves. Nobody else there but her and me. If we could just have done something so dreadful that they would have fled hell except us. (*SF*, 97)

In a conversation with his father, Quentin again expresses this desire: "It was to isolate her out of the loud world so that it would have to flee us of necessity and then the sound of it would be as though it had never been" (*SF*, 220). Similar words describe Satan's expulsion from Heaven:

> Hell heard th' unsufferable noise, Hell saw
> Heav'n ruining from Heav'n, and would have fled
> Affrighted: but strict Fate had cast too deep
> Her dark foundations, and too fast had bound.
> (*PL* VI.867–70)

Hell wants to flee but cannot, for even Hell is unable to escape the rule of Fate—that force which corresponds in Milton and in Faulkner to universal laws and is ultimately the will of God. In seeking to banish the world or to empty Hell, Quentin attempts a reversal of the natural order, in defiance of God. This aim, of course, also describes incest—both the act itself, which is a sin, and also what it signifies, that larger rebellion which is the Fall from God. Viewed in this light, Quentin's attraction to incest can scarcely be regarded, as some critics would have it, as a positive thing.[27]

Quentin's hostility is echoed in *As I Lay Dying* by Jewel Bundren whose defiance also takes the form of an incestuous love.[28] In a passage that is indebted, I believe, to Milton's well-known Sonnet XXVIII, Jewel envisions himself alone with his mother on a high hill—above, apart from, and against the world:[29]

> It would just be me and her on a high hill and me rolling the rocks down the hill at their faces, picking them up and throwing them down the hill faces and teeth and all by God until she was quiet and not that goddam adze going One lick less. (*AILD*, 15)

While Jewel's attachment to his mother is not overtly incestuous, it is certainly passionate, a fact evidenced in the sacrifice for her of his horse, his heroic actions to save the coffin, and also in the intensity of his jealousy of Cash. On her part Addie has loved her third son with a fierceness not vouchsafed her other children; and, if Cora Tull is to be believed, she has even allowed him to usurp the role of God, designating him "my cross" and "my salvation" who "will save me from the water and from the fire" (*AILD*, 160).

Incest results, in part, from a yearning for wholeness and oneness, but it can never satisfy this desire. Rather, it insures the very isolation it seeks to cure.[30] The incestuous partner, instead of reaching outward in love, turns inward upon the family and in effect attempts a union with a part of himself; such a pairing leads not to the communion that was desired but only a kind of self-communication. Quentin's terrible sense of isolation, his despair at the impossibility of communication, is captured vividly in the image of the two trains speeding past each other in the night: for an instant they meet; two faces appear in two opposed windows; and then they vanish in the darkness. As his narrative draws to a close, Quentin searches desperately for a door—a way out of his isolation, a way into the world—but it eludes him in the darkness.

Incest also appeals to Quentin as a way of halting time—of stopping the clock or even turning it back. It will, paradoxically, provide the means by which he will restore to Caddy the lost innocence of childhood; he will transform her moral transgressions into the sin of incest, assume himself the burden of guilt, and then wipe the slate clean.[31] Or, as Mr. Compson puts it, Quentin wants "to sublimate a piece of natural human folly into a horror and then exorcise it with truth" (*SF*, 220). Incest will also stop the clock for Quentin in providing the means whereby he will regain or acquire (in Caddy) a mother, something Quentin has never really had, as he himself tells us: "if I'd just had a mother so I could say Mother Mother" (*SF*, 213). Neurotic, selfish, and self-absorbed, Mrs. Compson has literally and figuratively removed herself from her family; much of her time is spent lying in bed with a camphor cloth to her head, her voice issuing plaintively "from behind the door." The extent of the parents' responsibility for their children's plight, at least in Quentin's eyes, is indicated in his haunting memory of a child's storybook picture: it reveals two dimly-lit faces "lifted out of the shadow" of a "dark place" which becomes, for Quentin, "the dungeon [that] was Mother herself she and Father upward into the weak light holding hands and us lost somewhere below even them without even a ray of light" (*SF*, 215). This passage summons scenes from *Paradise Lost*: the appearances of Adam and Eve in the garden, hand-in-hand; the plight of the fallen angels, submerged in the darkness of Hell; the promises of Satan and Beelzebub to obtain their followers' release, to "once more lift us up" within sight at least of Heaven's "bright confines" (*PL* II.393–95).[32] As Quentin evidently sees it, his parents, like Adam and Eve, have condemned not only themselves but also their children, and this sentence permits no escape; indeed, if the parallels with *Paradise Lost* hold true, any attempt will bring worse punishment and more woe.

Quentin's mournful lament for a mother is echoed in *As I Lay Dying* in Darl's laconic statement: "I cannot love my mother because I have no mother" (*AILD*, 89). Like Quentin, Darl has never known a real mother, and perhaps it is this void in his life which leads him, as it does Quentin, to establish with his sister a very special relationship.[33] Like Milton's Satan and Sin, whose hearts move together in "secret harmony," Dewey Dell and Darl "knowed things betwixt them"; that is, tuned in to one another in some mysterious way that does not require words, each is able to perceive the other's unspoken thoughts. There is little harmony in the relationship, but this is probably owing, too, to Darl's incestuous feelings for Dewey Dell; he taunts her with his knowledge that she is carrying Lafe's child because he is jealous of Lafe just as he is jealous of Jewel's relationship with Addie. That Darl desires Dewey Dell is indicated, certainly, by the sexual context in which he regards his sister. He strips her naked with his eyes; he observes beneath her wet and clinging dress "those mammalian ludicrosities which are the horizons and the valleys of the earth"; he takes note of "her leg coming long from beneath her tightening dress: that lever which moves the world; one of that caliper which measures the length and breadth of life" (*AILD*, 156, 97–98). The metaphor of the caliper, however, has been particularly misunderstood. It has been found to denote a "mechanized sexuality," a purging of "sexual passion," and the dehumanization of Dewey Dell.[34] But it is precisely as an instrument of creation, a symbol of fecundity, that Darl regards Dewey Dell, an attitude suggested by this passage's resemblance to one in *Paradise Lost*—Milton's description of the beginnings of the world:[35]

> Then stay'd the fervid Wheels, and in his hand
> He took the golden Compasses, prepar'd
> In God's Eternal store, to circumscribe
> This Universe, and all created things:
> One foot he centred, and the other turn'd
> Round through the vast profundity obscure,
> And said, Thus far extend, thus far thy bounds,
> This be thy just Circumference, O World.
> (*PL* VII.224–231)

Quentin too is drawn sexually to his sister, his attraction to Caddy most apparent in his recollection of an incident at the branch. In this scene Quentin opens his knife and places it against Caddy's throat, and then the two converse in a passage that is fraught with sexual implications:

it won't take but a second Ill try not to hurt
all right
will you close your eyes
no like this youll have to push it harder
touch your hand to it
but she didnt move her eyes were wide open looking
      past my head at the sky
Caddy do you remember how Dilsey fussed at you
      because your drawers were muddy
don't cry
Im not crying Caddy
push it are you going to
do you want me to
yes push it
touch your hand to it
dont cry poor Quentin. (*SF*, 189)

The knife of course functions in this passage as a phallic symbol, as weapons often do in the works of Faulkner, a use which is repeated, more clearly and plainly, in *The Wild Palms*. As Harry prepares to abort their child, Charlotte says to him, " 'We've done this lots of ways but not with knives, have we?' " Earlier, after asking Harry " 'Does it matter who you do it on?,' " she confesses to confusing abortion with incest. Perhaps thoughts of incest occur naturally to Charlotte because she is no stranger to them. Born into a family that very much resembles in its organization those in *The Sound and the Fury* and *As I Lay Dying,* Charlotte has developed an unusually—and unnaturally—strong attachment to one of her brothers. At their first meeting she tells Harry:

> "all my family were brothers except me. I liked my oldest brother the best but you cant sleep with your brother and he and Rat roomed together in school so I married Rat."[36]

Quentin, however, is also revolted by the instincts that he finds so compelling, an attitude which may owe something to his dependence on Caddy and his fear of losing her but which probably stems more from the effort to suppress his own incestuous desires. Frequently—or usually— sex appears to Quentin as dirty and ugly. He associates it with the "stinking" yellow mud of the hog wallow, with the cloying, too-sweet smell of honeysuckle, with swine "in pairs rushing coupled into the sea," with "nigger women . . . in the pasture the ditches the dark woods" (*SF*, 113–14, 219). Caddy is linked in his imagination with the little Italian girl, whose pigtails, dirty clothes, coffee-colored skin, and obscene loaf of bread all indicate, for Quentin, an innocence defiled. The extent of Quentin's revulsion is evident in his thoughts of self-mutilation and in his desire for an innocence that is beyond castration, that is, "never to have had them" (*SF,* 143).

Quentin's ambivalence in sexual matters is found in other Faulkner characters too. Horace Benbow of *Flags in the Dust* is one. Another is Sir Galwyn of *Mayday,* a knight-errant who is accompanied in his travels by two allegorical characters, Hunger and Pain. Hunger, "with a hundred prehensile mouths," and Pain, "with a hundred restless hands," pull and tug at Sir Galwyn until at last he escapes them both in the watery embrace of Little Sister Death. Similarly, Quentin is flanked on one side by Jason, his hands jammed compulsively in his pockets, and on the other side by Benjy, his mouth open in whimpering anticipation of the spoon. These two attitudes are most vividly represented in *The Wild Palms* and *Old Man*; two stories published under one cover in alternating chapters, they present in counterpoint two opposing themes: the sacrifice of everything in life, even life itself, for love; and the attempt to escape, at any cost, its demands and griefs.

This inner tug-of-war renders Quentin emotionally, and perhaps physically, impotent.[37] His paralysis is demonstrated plainly in the scene at the branch, where he fumbles ineffectually for the misplaced knife as Caddy, losing interest, rises to leave. In a conversation with his father, Quentin admits that he never tried to make Caddy commit incest, for fear that she would: "i was afraid to i was afraid she might" (*SF,* 220).[38] His fears, moreover, are not groundless, as Caddy's declaration to her brother at the branch reveals: "I'll do anything you want me to anything yes" (*SF,* 220). This admission elicits a violent response from Quentin, who shakes her and tells her to "shut up." Some critics believe that Quentin would have fared better had he actually committed incest for that would be a significant action, but this interpretation, I believe, ignores the ugliness of incest and assumes that for Faulkner, as for Eliot, the greatest sin is sloth.

The dangers that Quentin runs in repressing his instinctual life are recognized by Mr. Compson, who tells his son that it is nature, not Caddy, that is hurting him. Quentin, however, seems unable to absorb the lesson that the instinctual self will not be denied, that normal and healthy impulses, when consistently rejected, have a way of exacting their revenge.[39] It is a failure for which Quentin pays dearly. The emotional and psychological scars he carries are represented symbolically by the broken leg he suffers in the fall from the horse, an animal that frequently stands for male potency in Faulkner's works. In Quentin's mind, however, the accident remains linked with Caddy's promiscuity and her need to marry. In *As I Lay Dying* is found a counterpart to Quentin's twice broken leg: the leg which Cash breaks twice, first in the fall from the roof of a church and then in a fall from the wagon in the fording of the river. Like Quentin, Darl seems to associate the accident with his sister's moral fall and, additionally, to regard Cash as some sort of victim, as perhaps paying the price for Dewey Dell's "compulsions," those "weary gestures wearily recapitulant" (*AILD*, 196–97).

It is not surprising then that Quentin, given his fear and revulsion of sex, should aspire to a merging of minds and souls, not a union of bodies. It is a spiritual incest he hankers after, one that recalls, in its desire for complete possession and its penchant for self-destruction, the incestuous love of Roderick and Madeline Usher. In his essay on Poe, D. H. Lawrence describes the deadliness of such a love:

> In sensual love, it is the two blood-systems, the man's and the woman's, which sweep up into pure contact, and *almost* fuse. Almost mingle. Never quite. There is always the finest imaginable wall between the two blood-waves, through which pass unknown vibrations, forces, but through which the blood itself must never break, or it means bleeding.
>
> In spiritual love, the contact is purely nervous. The nerves in the lovers are set vibrating in unison like two instruments. The pitch can rise higher and higher. But carry this too far, and the nerves begin to break, to bleed, as it were, and a form of death sets in.
>
> The trouble about man is that he insists on being the master of his own fate, and he insists on *oneness*.[40]

Incest, then, provides the near-perfect vehicle for the effort to possess absolutely and to achieve complete oneness: "Two persons of the least dissimilarity offer the least physical resistance to mutual participation in the *fire* of a common being."[41] Only the hermaphrodite, incorporating within himself the male and female principles in unobstructed union, can serve as a better metaphor. Yet this form of narcissism proves no more satisfactory than that of incest; in *Mosquitoes* Eva Wiseman's poem describes the grief that ensues:

> "Weary thy mouth with smiling; canst thou bride
> Thyself with thee and thine own kissing slake?
> Thy virgin's waking doth itself deride
> With sleep's sharp absence, coming so awake,
> And near thy mouth thy twinned heart's grief doth hide
> For there's no breast between: it cannot break."
> (*M*, 252)

What Quentin yearns for is angelic love—pure, unbounded, unimpeded; but such a love is not permitted to man, not even in Milton's Paradise.

The wholeness and oneness that has eluded Quentin in incest, he now seeks in death, an end he desires as fervently as a lover longs for his mistress:[42]

> But who loved death above all, who loved only death, loved and lived in a deliberate and almost perverted anticipation of death as a lover loves and deliberately refrains from the waiting willing friendly tender incredible body of his beloved, until he can no longer bear not the refraining but the restraint and so flings, hurls himself, relinquishing, drowning. (*SFA*, 411)

Like Emily Grierson who literally embraces death, or like Rougemont's courtly lovers who "demand a union so absolute that their bodies become a hindrance," Quentin can find only in death "the perfect consummation" of love.[43] But Quentin has not forsaken incest in courting oblivion; when the figure in the water merges with that of Caddy to become Little Sister Death, the incestuous union is truly death's embrace.[44] In seeking the completeness every man desires, Quentin is simply demonstrating "all the longing of mankind for a Oneness with Something, somewhere"; the irony is that he should pursue it in incest and death, themselves the symbols of man's fall from wholeness (*SP*, 319).

In contrast to Benjy, Quentin is clearly the postlapsarian Adam, a man trapped in the hiatus between the Fall and the redemption. Like Adam, he is obsessed with the world's evil, particularly on the last day of his life. The imagery which commands his attention then—the hour of noon, forms of slanting light, the repeated appearances of his shadow—recalls images of the Fall in *Paradise Lost*: the time of Eve's temptation, the tilting of the earth on its axis after the Fall, the figure of the shadow-like Death. Tormented by what he sees as corruption and anxious, like Adam and Eve, to evade the penalties of the Fall, Quentin casts about in his mind for some means of escape, settling at length on two of the propositions posited by Eve: sexual abstinence and suicide. While Adam however rejects these evasions, which will "provoke the Highest / To make death in us live," Quentin embraces the ultimate solution (*PL*, X.1027–28). He regards death as a haven, a path to Eden, seeing in the peaceful "grottoes and caverns" of the sea that will receive him the very "grots and caves" of Milton's Paradise. In this, however, Quentin is clearly mistaken; the bridge that witnesses his death, "arching slow and high into space" like the "high Archt" bridge built by Sin and Death, leads not to Heaven (*SF*, 212; *PL*, X.301).

Jason, the third of the Compson sons to narrate the family's story, embodies Milton's faculty of reason. He is "logical, rational, contained," the "first sane Compson since before Culloden," but he is "logical" and "sane" primarily in the sense that he represents the head as opposed to the heart (*SFA*, 420). He is, certainly, a far cry from the "virtue," "freedom," "conscience," and "being of soul" which characterize Milton's right reason. He illustrates instead the disharmony that can result when the hierarchy of the faculties is disturbed, when the authority of right reason is usurped by a lower faculty such as passion: then reason can "dictate false, and misinform the Will / To Do what God expressly hath forbid" (*PL* IX.355–56). And it is clear that Jason, although a logical man, is scarcely a dispassionate one. He is buffeted and driven by a wide array of emotions: fury, greed, envy, vengeance, despair—all, it seems, save love. He is a cold cruel man, and Caddy is right when she tells him, "You never had a drop of warm blood in you" (*SF*, 259).

Like his brothers, Jason falls prey to incestuous feelings, but his longings attach themselves to Caddy's daughter, Quentin. While he certainly does not admit to incestuous impulses and, in all likelihood, does not recognize them for what they are, Jason unwittingly reveals himself to the reader. He demonstrates his sexual interest in his niece in verbal attacks that dwell angrily and jealously on her laxness. He calls her a bitch, a slut, and a whore, refers to her bad blood, calls attention to her nakedness, and likens her to the women "on Gayoso or Beale street." His obsession with Quentin's exploits rivals even his brother's preoccupation with Caddy's amorous adventures. Jason's relationship with his niece, in fact, parallels that of Quentin and Caddy in many respects, a correspondence which supports the argument of Jason's incestuous feelings. The verbal resemblances in the two monologues are especially notable: in each one, the woman is referred to as a whore, accused of hiding in the woods, and scorned for acting like "nigger women," while the suitor is designated a "squirt" and a "drummer." Certain similarities of attitude are also present: anger and jealousy at Caddy's and Quentin's sexual involvement with other men, and "an unmistakable touch of prurience and voyeurism" in the Compson brothers' pursuit of the women and their lovers. Additionally, there is "between Quentin's sense of honor and Jason's concern for respectability . . . only a difference of degree."[45]

Like Quentin, Jason tries to repress his incestuous feelings. He gives vent instead to a very different set of emotions: anger, resentment, bitterness, and even hatred—feelings whose intensity indicates, though, "the depth of his emotional involvement."[46] One indication of the control Jason has always maintained over certain areas of feeling is his habit, as a child, of keeping his hands buried tightly in his pockets—a compulsion that links him with another Faulkner character associated with repression: *Mayday*'s Pain and his "hundred restless hands." A habitual concern with the hands is peculiar also to Wing Biddlebaum, of Sherwood Anderson's

Winesburg, Ohio; he too keeps his restless hands hidden away in his pockets, lest they expose his "hunger" to express his love of man.[47]

Jason is also related to the figure of Pain and the idea of repression by the anguish of the headaches he suffers, but these headaches link Jason primarily with Milton's Satan and the Fall. At the gates of Hell in *Paradise Lost*, Sin recapitulates for Satan the story of her birth and the history of their relationship:

> Hast thou forgot me then, and do I seem
> Now in thine eyes so foul, once deem'd so fair
> In Heav'n, when at th' Assembly, and in sight
> Of all the Seraphim with thee combin'd
> In Bold conspiracy against Heav'n's King,
> All on a sudden miserable pain
> Surpris'd thee, dim thine eyes, and dizzy swum
> In darkness, while thy head flames thick and fast
> Threw forth, till on the left side op'ning wide,
> Likest to thee in shape and count'nance bright
> Then shining heav'nly fair, a Goddess arm'd
> Out of thy head I sprung: amazement seiz'd
> All th' Host of Heav'n; back they recoil'd afraid
> At first, and call'd me *Sin*, and for a Sign
> Portentous held me; but familiar grown,
> I pleas'd, and with attractive graces won
> The most averse, thee chiefly, who full oft
> Thyself in me thy perfect image viewing
> Becam'st enamor'd, and such joy thou took'st
> With me in secret, that my womb conceiv'd
> A growing burden. Meanwhile War arose,
> And fields were fought in Heav'n: wherein remain'd
> (For what could else) to our Almighty Foe
> Clear Victory, to our part loss and rout
> Through all Empyrean: down they fell
> Driv'n headlong from the Pitch of Heaven, down
> Into this Deep, and in the general fall
> I also. . . . (*PL* II.747–774)

Many of the elements in this story find their way into the account of Jason and his headaches. Jason's pain, like Satan's, is severe: he feels as if his head may split, "explode," or "burst" (*SF,* 297). His attack, like Satan's, is almost blinding and comes upon him suddenly. His pain also is closely associated with the incestuous partner, becoming most acute during those mad forays in pursuit of Quentin and her drummer.[48] While the headache's pain does not, in Jason's case, as in Satan's, announce the arrival of a daughter, Jason does feel as if "somebody was inside with a hammer, beating on it," and he does play a parental part in relation to Quentin, a role clearly recognized by Mrs. Compson when she reminds Quentin,

"He is the nearest thing to a father you've ever had" (*SF*, 297, 324). And finally, in Jason's case too the pain of the headache is rooted in pride; much of his fury as he tears after his niece derives from an obsessive concern wtih reputation and status, from his perception of Quentin as a blot on the family's honor.

In Jason, as in Satan, this pride unites with envy to fuel the revolt against God. Satan's jealousy of man, one aspect of his envy, is best revealed on the two occasions when his efforts to enter Eden are halted, temporarily, by the "wilderness . . . with thicket overgrown"; "so thick entwin'd / As one continu'd brake, the undergrowth / Of shrubs and tangling bushes" that, for the moment, all access is barred (*PL* IV.135–36, 174–76). In *The Sound and the Fury*, Jason encounters a similar wilderness ringing his Eden; a "heavy underbrush" becoming "thicker and thicker" impedes his progress to Quentin's tryst with her drummer. Like the thicket of *Paradise Lost*, it boasts a serpent, introduced in Jason's comparison of poison ivy to a snake and present particularly in the person of Jason, who is compelled by the brambles to "twist around" and "wind around" to such an extent that he almost loses his way in the woods. These gyrations bring to mind the prelude to the temptation: Satan's search "through each Thicket, Dank or Dry" for the serpent whose "mazy folds" will hide him and his discovery, finally, of the sleeping reptile "In Labyrinth of many a round self-roll'd" (*PL* IX.161–62, 179–83). The comparison emphasizes not only Jason's desire for his niece, whom he would seduce if he could, but also his responsibility for her fall, the part played by his cruelty and abuse.

Jason is, of course, a satanic figure in many respects.[49] Like Satan, he is a good hater, lashing out at "damn eastern jews," rednecks, blacks, and women. He too suffers from a "sense of injur'd merit," resenting bitterly Quentin's year at Harvard and the banking job that Caddy cost him. He is a cruel, arrogant, and angry man—a liar, a thief, and a hypocrite, absolutely without conscience. But as we have noted, in his abuse of his niece Jason demonstrates most explicitly his affinities with evil. He reveals, in addition to envy and pride, a thirst for revenge in his relationship with Quentin, whom he regards as the very symbol of lost opportunities.[50] It is a vengefulness, moreover, that is emblematic of an even greater madness: a hatred of Heaven itself. As he pursues Quentin to Mottson, Jason identifies, in a most Miltonic passage, the true source of his anger:

From time to time he passed churches, unpainted frame buildings with sheet iron steeples, surrounded by tethered teams and shabby motorcars, and it seemed to him that each of them was a picket-post where the rear guards of Circumstance peeped fleetingly back at him. "And damn You, too," he said, "See if You can stop me," thinking of himself, his file of soldiers with the manacled sheriff in the rear, dragging Omnipotence down from His throne, if necessary; of the embattled legions of both hell and heaven through which he tore his way and put his hands at last on his fleeing niece. (*SF,* 382)

And in Jason's case, as in Satan's, the evil redounds upon itself; as old Job tells Jason (who is, like Satan, the "accuser" of Job), he is so clever that he outwits himself.

But Jason's relationship with Quentin is less like Satan's with Sin and more like Satan's with Eve in one respect: the enmity between the two. In the hope of encouraging a better relationship, Mrs. Compson reminds Quentin of her obligations to Jason: "It's his bread you and I eat" (*SF,* 324). In the Compson household, however, there is little breaking of bread, in the sense of a sharing of affection or even the simple joining together in a communal activity. For Jason and Quentin the dinner table serves as a battleground where Jason baits and torments his niece, while Quentin, looking like a cornered animal, crumbles her untasted biscuit into her plate. In Jason's eyes, the bread they eat is a worthless commodity, of such low value that the measure of his scorn for the curative powers of aspirin is to compare it to bread. Bread also figures prominently in the scenes featuring Quentin and the little coffee-colored Italian girl, whom he calls sister, and it points to no communion there; the baker of the bread is cold and unkind, and the bread itself is associated with images of ugliness and death. Of all the family, only Dilsey—pictured repeatedly at the bread board, working and singing—is able to establish a communion with others that the bread seems to symbolize.

The absence of communion and, sometimes, even that of communication is characteristic of the incestuous relationship.[51] The incest results, in part, from the isolation of the family members, and then it perpetuates the condition from which it sprang. The sense of isolation which pervades the Compson household is conveyed by a number of images—fences, gates, and locks—but it is held primarily in the image of the door. Mrs. Compson speaks from beyond closed doors; Caddie stands within doors; Benjy sees doors as mirrors; Jason and his niece slam doors or lock them; Quentin searches for a door. Of all the Compsons, however, Jason is the most isolated, the most locked-in. He keeps his money—and where his treasure is his heart is also—in a locked box, under a section of floor planking, within a closet, inside his locked room. In contrast to the Compsons, Dilsey opens doors and walks through doorways. She is also pictured, repeatedly, mounting the stairs, an indication that her powers of communication extend in two directions: horizontally with her fellow man and vertically to God.

While Jason remains unmatched in the novel for sheer villainy, he is not the first Compson to revolt. Jason comes from a long line of rebels—failed rebels, men who were bold and daring but who were forced in the end to flee for their lives. One notable exception was Governor Quentin MacLachan, a man whose title seems to suggest a restraint, moderation, and control that was markedly lacking in the rest of the clan.[52] But by the time of Jason III, the father in *The Sound and the Fury,* even the courage had about played out. It appears again briefly in Caddy and her daughter, but these women too are doomed. Caddy is last seen consorting with a Nazi, her face "ageless and beautiful, cold, serene and damned"; Quentin vanishes in the company of a hard and flashy carnival man to follow what promises to be a tawdry and dissolute existence (*SFA,* 415). When she descends the pear tree to elope with the drummer, Quentin in a sense completes the action initiated by Caddy, so long ago, when she climbed that same tree to look on death. And yet Caddy, if not Quentin, is certainly a rebel of a different caliber from Jason; described by her creator as "the beautiful one" and "my heart's darling," she is drawn with great sympathy and understanding.[53] And she, more than Jason, demonstrates the uses to which even wickedness can be put: "That all this good of evil shall produce, / And evil turn to good" (*PL* XII.470–71). In an address at Pine Manor, Faulkner puts it plainly:

> So God used the dark spirit too. He did not merely cast it shrieking out of the universe, as He could have done. Instead, He used it. He already presaw the long roster of ambition's ruthless avatars—Genghis and Caesar and William and Hitler and Barca and Stalin and Bonaparte and Huey Long. But he used more—not only the ambition and the ruthlessness and the arrogance to show man what to revolt against, but also the temerity to revolt and the will to change what one does not like.[54]

The fourth section of the novel, narrated by the author himself, focuses primarily on Dilsey, who presents an alternative to the Compson way of life. Dilsey is the "one just man," "fearless of reproach and scorn / Or violence" who will show us "the paths of righteousness" (*PL* XI.811–14). Her function is made apparent immediately, in the first part of this section, where her story is given a symbolic content that relates it to the history of all mankind: the creation, the fall, damnation or redemption. First, the description of Dilsey's entrance into the light of the new day suggests, in the Miltonic images, the story of the earth's beginning:

> The day dawned bleak and chill, a moving wall of grey light out of the northeast which, instead of dissolving into moisture, seemed to distintegrate into minute and venomous particles, like dust that, when Dilsey opened the door of the cabin and emerged, needled laterally into her flesh, precipitating not so much a moisture as a substance partaking of the quality of thin, not quite congealed oil. (*SF,* 330)

In Raphael's story of the earth's creation—his description of the mountains emerging and the water fleeing into the valleys—many of the same images appear:

> thither they
> Hasted with glad precipitance, uproll'd
> As drops on dust conglobing from the dry;
> Part rise in crystal Wall, or ridge direct,
> For haste. . . .
> And on the washy Ooze deep Channels wore. . . .
> (*PL* VII.290–94, 303)

Dilsey's portrait also contains images denoting the Fall:

> The gown fell gauntly . . . across her fallen breasts, then tightened upon her paunch and fell again, ballooning a little above the nether garments . . . in color regal and moribund . . . the indomitable skeleton was left rising like a ruin . . . above the collapsed face. (*SF,* 330–31)

In the third paragraph, the imagery turns hellish with the appearance of the jaybirds—raucous, infernal creatures that "came up from nowhere, whirled up on the blast like gaudy scraps of cloth or paper" (*SF,* 331).[55] But there are also suggestions of redemption: the rain anointing Dilsey's skin like oil; the indomitable skeleton rising above the decay. For Dilsey offers an alternative to the Hell the Compsons inhabit; pictured repeatedly in the novel mounting the stairs, working at the bread board, opening doors and entering rooms, Dilsey introduces the possibilities of leading a life that is full and rich in the service of both man and God.

For much of this section, though, it is the Fall that is stressed; the realities of the Compson world are finally and fully revealed. In the descriptions of the house and grounds—the "shabby garden" and "broken fence," "the square, paintless house with its rotting portico," the ticking of the clock like "the dry pulse of the decaying house itself"—images of death and decay abound (*SF,* 360, 372, 355). The story of the theft of Jason's money—Quentin shinnying up the pear tree, entering through the window, and breaking open the multiplicity of locks and bolts—suggests Satan's easy and contemptuous entrance into Eden:

> Or as a Thief bent to unhoard the cash
> Of some rich Burgher, whose substantial doors,
> Cross-barr'd and bolted fast, fear no assault,
> In at the window climbs, or o'er the tiles:
> So clomb this first grand Thief into God's Fold . . .
> (*PL* IV.188–92)

The descriptions of Quentin's abandoned room—its emptiness, the scraping and rasping of the pear tree against the house, the "forlorn scent of blossoms"—summon memories of the Fall: the fallen angels' "vacant room" in Heaven, the apple tree in Paradise, Eden's "wild woods Forlorn."[56] Another fallen garden is found in Mottson beside the railroad station, a spot where "grass grew rigidly in a plot bordered with rigid flowers and a sign in electric lights: Keep your [eye] on Mottson, the gap filled by a human eye with an electric pupil" (*SF*, 388). It is a parody of Milton's Paradise, where the "eye of the World," the sun, shines benevolently on the "two of Mankind" in the "Garden-Plot" of Eden.[57]

The image of the hill, in this section, points also to the Fall. On the final leg of his journey into Mottson, Jason climbs a hill, pauses a moment, and then makes the descent into the valley below:

> He crested the final hill. Smoke lay in the valley, and roofs, a spire or two above trees. He drove down the hill and into the town. . . . He could not see very well now, and he knew that it was the disaster which kept telling him to go directly and get something for his head. (*SF*, 384)

The Negro church where Dilsey takes Benjy to the Easter service rests on the summit of a hill. Perched above the shabby Negro houses that sit on littered grassless plots amid sad spring-forgotten trees, it raises its "crazy steeple" against the sky, presenting a scene as flat and devoid of perspective "as a painted cardboard set upon the ultimate edge of the flat earth" (*SF*, 364). Earlier, in Benjy's narrative, the image of the hill appears in his recollections of the incident with the Burgess girl, his memory of the terrible sensation of falling: "I tried to keep from falling off the hill, and I fell off the hill into the bright whirling shapes" (*SF*, 64).

These passages hearken back to "The Hill," a sketch published in *The Mississippian* in 1922. On his way home at the end of the day's work, a laborer climbs a hill and pauses at the top to look at the valley below and reflect:

> His long shadow legs rose perpendicularly and fell, ludicrously, as though without power of progression, as though his body had been mesmerized by a whimsical God to a futile puppet-like activity upon one spot. . . . At last his shadow reached the crest and fell headlong over it. . . . The entire valley stretched beneath him, and his shadow, springing far out, lay across it, quiet and enormous. Here and there a thread of smoke balanced precariously upon a chimney. . . . Behind him was a day of harsh labor with his hands, a strife against the forces of nature to gain bread and clothing and a place to sleep, a victory gotten at the price of bodily tissues and the numbered days of his existence. . . . The sun plunged silently into the liquid green of the west and the valley was abruptly in shadow. . . . Behind him was the motionless conflagration of sunset, before him was the opposite valley rim upon the changing sky. For a while he stood

on one horizon and stared across at the other, far above the world of endless toil and troubled slumber; untouched, untouchable; forgetting, for a space, that he must return. . . . He slowly descended the hill.[58]

These images of "The Hill" remained with Faulkner, finding their way eventually into most of the novels. Some of them he brought to the writing of his first book, *Soldier's Pay*; at the close of the novel, the rector and Joe Gilligan crest a hill, from which they see "the world breaking away from them into dark moon-silvered ridges above valleys where mist hung slumbrous." It is the fallen world they view, a "mooned land inevitable with to-morrow and sweat, with sex and death and damnation" (*SP,* 318, 319).

Similar imagery appears in *Mayday,* where it is used to describe the act of love:

and time and eternity swirled up and vortexed about the rush of their falling and the earth was but a spinning bit of dust in a maelstrom of blue space. . . . Young Sir Galwyn was no longer afraid: never had his heart known such ecstasy! he was a god and a falling star. . . .[59]

The identification of the Fall with the sexual act, however, is made most explicit in *The Wild Palms,* where Harry Wilbourne compares the loss of virginity with a plunge over the "dark precipice":

you are one single abnegant affirmation, one single fluxative Yes out of the terror in which you surrender volition, hope, all—the darkness, the falling, the thunder of solitude, the shock, the death, the moment when, stopped physically by the ponderable clay, you yet feel all your life rush out of you into the pervading immemorial blind receptive matrix, the hot fluid blind foundation—grave-womb or womb-grave, it's all one. (*WP,* 138)[60]

In *The Hamlet* the concept of death predominates as Ike and the cow, at day's end, make the descent from Paradise:

Joined by the golden skein of the wet grass rope, they move in single file toward the ineffable effulgence, directly into the sun. They are still pacing it. They mount the final ridge. They will arrive together. At the same moment all three of them cross the crest and descend into the bowl of evening and are extinguished. (*H,* 185)

Images of the Fall—the hill or precipice, the hiatus, and then the plunge—abound in *As I Lay Dying.* They are found in Jewel's vision of Addie and himself removed to "a high hill," in the "black void" Dewey Dell senses beneath her, in Darl's sighting of the dead mules between "two hills" of water, and in the comparison of Dewey Dell's breasts to "the horizons and valleys of the earth." They appear in Darl's description of Jewel mounting his horse: the "illusion" of "wings" in the whirling hooves, Jewel's snake-like limberness as he is jerked "earth-free," the "rigid terrific hiatus," and then the descent from the hill. The Bundrens' travels, a metaphor for the journey through life, commence with a fall, the descent from the bluff on which their house perches precariously, "tilting a little down the hill." The journey concludes as the family tops the final hill on the outskirts of Jefferson, where Darl describes the scene below: "From the crest of a hill . . . we can see the smoke low and flat, seemingly unmoving in the unwinded afternoon"; above, the buzzards "hang in narrowing circles, like the smoke, with an outward semblance of form and purpose, but with no inference of motion, progress or retrograde." Then the final descent is made, and the voyage through the waters of Chaos and the fires of Hell concludes with a burial at the cemetery. It is a journey endlessly repeated and one that, in Darl's eyes, is ultimately without direction and meaning (*AILD*, 156, 12, 19, 216).

These images in Faulkner of the hill or precipice, the ascent and the fall, recall similar imagery in *Paradise Lost*. In Book XI Michael guides Adam to the summit of the highest hill of Paradise and there unfolds for him the future of all mankind. It is a story of "good with bad," one of "supernal Grace contending / With sinfulness of Men" (*PL* XI.358–60). In Book XII Michael and Adam "descend" the "top of Speculation" under the watchful eyes of angelic guards on a neighboring hill; next the cherubim themselves wind their way down the hill; and then Adam and Eve make the final descent from Eden:

> and from the other Hill
> To thir fixt Station, all in bright array
> The Cherubim descended; on the ground
> Gliding meteorous, as Ev'ning Mist
> Ris'n from a River o'er the marish glides,
> And gathers ground fast at the Laborer's heel
> Homeward returning. . . .
> In either hand the hast'ning Angel caught
> Our ling'ring Parents, and to th' Eastern Gate
> Led them direct, and down the Cliff as fast
> To the subject Plain; then disappear'd.
> (*PL* XII.626–32, 637–40)

In Milton's epic, the role of the hill or cliff is clear; it witnesses the descent into the world of time and history, the fall into toil, sex, pain, and death. In Faulkner's works, the significance of these images, although not so readily apparent, remains the same.

The conclusion of *The Sound and the Fury* has been the source of some puzzlement for its readers and the subject of a good deal of critical conjecturing. It has been seen to epitomize the violence of the book, to expose again the Compson sin of pride, and to reveal the persistence in the present of the false values of the past: observations which are on track but do not go quite far enough.[61] What the final segment of *The Sound and the Fury* epitomizes—what the novel all along has been about— is the Fall of man, and more specifically, the Fall of the Southern man. The presence of the monument to the Confederate soldier is an immediate reminder of the Civil War and the South's original sin, its enslavement of the black man. The arrogance and pride which characterized Southern rule is demonstrated in the decision of Luster, although he is black, to "show dem niggers how quality does" (*SF*, 399). The violence of white against black and of man against his brother erupts again as Jason strikes first Luster and then Ben. The elements of death and damnation, the inevitable results of the Fall for both man and region, are present in Jason's orders to Luster: "Get to hell on home with him. If you ever cross that gate with him again, I'll kill you!" (*SF*, 400). When Jason's anger, at this point, joins with Benjy's wailing, this scene does indeed become "the novel's most intense depiction of sound and fury."[62]

The Fall is indicated particularly in the conclusion by the role that Benjy plays. As he rides behind the ancient white horse (recalling in Milton Death's "pale Horse"), her "gait resembling a prolonged and suspended fall," Benjy clutches a mended narcissus. It is a bloom which is emblematic not only of Benjy but of the entire Compson family as well, pointing especially to the willfulness of Caddy.[63] Recalling the flowers of Paradise and Eve's diligence in propping with myrtle bands the blossom whose "head . . . Hung drooping unsustain'd," Benjy's splinted narcissus underscores Caddy's abandonment of him; his flower is repaired not by his sister but by Luster, and as his perpetually bobbing head suggests, he is terribly in need of Caddy's support (*PL* IX.428–30).[64] Unhappily, however, Caddy was herself without a prop; and as a result, like Milton's "fairest unsupported Flow'r," she too was "defac't, deflow'r'd" (*PL* IX.432; IX.901).

Benjy's misery, also, points to the Fall and the anguish it brings into the world. His entrapment in the physical world of the idiot—"It was as if even eagerness were muscle-bound in him too and hunger itself inarticulate"—suggests Adam's grief at the news that he must quit Paradise: the "sorrow" that "all his senses bound" (*SF*, 344–45; *PL* XI.264–65). At the close of the novel, when Luster turns left at the monument, Benjy registers vocally this cosmic grief: "There was more than astonishment in it, it was horror; shock; agony eyeless, tongueless; just sound" (*SF*, 400). He is Adam confronting the fallen Eve: "amaz'd" "Astonied,"

"Blank," "Speechless," and "pale," "while horror chill / Ran through his veins" (*PL* IX.889–94). Another detail in this scene which is significant, perhaps, is Faulkner's use of the turn to the left to trigger Benjy's outburst; if it refers to Milton's association of left with Eve, the product of Adam's "part sinister," or with Sin who emerges from the left of Satan's head, then this scene makes a very strong statement about Caddy's role in the family's demise.

The crux of the conclusion's problems however lies in its restoration of peace and order. At the novel's close, Luster drives Benjy back home:

> The broken flower drooped over Ben's fist and his eyes were empty and blue and serene again as cornice and facade flowed smoothly once more from left to right; post and tree, window and doorway, and sign-board, each in its ordered place. (*SF,* 401)

This scene is interpreted, generally, as one that appears to be felicitous but is not; the harmony, which is restored by the book's villain and is achieved in the mind of an idiot, is found to be "empty," "static," "sterile," and meaningless.[65]

A look at this passage, however, in the light of *Paradise Lost* goes far, I believe, to illuminate Faulkner's intentions: a reading that is not ironical. While we concede that peace is achieved in the mind of an idiot, we recall that, according to Milton (and also Corinthians), God often selects a curious vehicle for his grace—and that this theory of inversion is put to work often in Faulkner's works.[66] At the conclusion of Book XII, Adam explains what he knows now to be his duty:

> and by small
> Accomplishing great things, by things deem'd weak
> Subverting worldly strong, and worldly wise
> By simply meek . . . (*PL* XII.566–69)

And if order is restored at the hands of a villain, that too is not inexplicable; a major theme of *Paradise Lost* is the concept that evil is often the unwilling and unwitting instrument of good.

But the strongest argument for a straightforward interpretation of Faulkner's passage is its similarity to several in *Paradise Lost* celebrating a restoration of order, control, harmony, and balance. In Book I, in the midst of the turmoil of Hell, the rule of the "Scepter'd Angels" is recalled: "Each in his Hierarchy, the Orders bright" (I.737). In a description of the creation in Book III, Uriel pictures the world's emergence from chaos:

> I saw when at his Word the formless Mass,
> This world's material mould, came to a heap:

> Confusion heard his voice, and wild uproar
> Stood rul'd, stood vast infinitude confin'd;
> Till at this second bidding darkness fled,
> Light shone, and order from disorder sprung:
> Swift to thir several Quarters hasted then
> The cumbrous Elements, Earth, Flood, Air, Fire,
> And this Ethereal quintessence of Heav'n
> Flew upward, spirited with various forms,
> That roll'd orbicular, and turn'd to Stars
> Numberless, as thou seest, and how they move;
> Each had his place appointed, each his course
> The rest in circuit walls this Universe.
> (*PL* III.707–21)

In Book VI we see a return to order as the messiah takes charge of the armies of God in the War of Heaven: "At his command the uprooted Hills retir'd / Each to his place" (VI.781–82). Book XI witnesses the resumption, after the Flood, of control and balance in the natural world:

> Day and Night,
> Seed-time and Harvest, Heat and hoary Frost
> Shall hold their course. . . . (*PL* XI.898–900)

Similar words are employed in "The Bear" to present the timeless, immutable march of the seasons: "summer, and fall, and snow, and saprife spring in their ordered immortal sequence."[67]

Not only are the verbal resemblances striking but also the similar places the passages occupy in the works—each occurring at or near the end of a book or a chapter to celebrate the return to order from disorder. If the harmony is destined to be short-lived, as that in *The Sound and the Fury* doubtlessly will be, it is no less real; in the long history of man, periods of peace have always been brief and rare, as Michael's forecast in XI and XII reveals. If the Compson family is doomed, Dilsey and Benjy will endure; and we recall that it is people, not clans or dynasties, that Faulkner cherishes.

The progression of landmarks—"post and tree, window and doorway, and sign-board"—also signals the choices we face: death and life, rejection or acceptance. It is the same purpose served by incest; in its function as a metaphor for original sin, it impresses upon us the ugliness of evil, alerts us to the need for change, and warns of impending harm. In *The Sound and the Fury,* where the theme pervades all four sections of the book and includes all five of the Compson progeny, incest points to the pride, arrogance, and solipsism that lie deep in the Compson clan and eventually destroy it.

4

Absalom, Absalom!

Published in 1936 and marking the conclusion of the great period of creativity that began with *Flags in the Dust* and *The Sound and the Fury*, *Absalom, Absalom!* differs from the earlier works in several respects—its scope and grandeur, its rhetoric and intensity. The thematic concerns of the book, however, remain the same as before.[1] In *Absalom, Absalom!* Faulkner focuses his attention again on the demise of a once-proud Southern family, and he once again identifies this end, more explicitly though, with the defeat of the South—both collapses pointing as before to the original Fall. Here too man's Fall is signalled by incest, a theme that pervades the entire novel and touches virtually every member of the Sutpen family. Denoting the arrogant pride in the Southern character and pointing to a disintegration in the individual and society, it alerts us to wrongs that have been committed and warns of impending ruin.

The theme of incest in *Absalom, Absalom!* is found primarily in the relationship of Judith, Henry, and Bon, a highly complex triangular arrangement in which each of the Sutpens is incestuously involved with the other two siblings. Of these relationships, the one most critical to the action of the novel and also most likely to develop into actual incest is that of Charles Bon and his half-sister, Judith. It is also the most puzzling to narrators and readers alike. Little is actually known of this courtship, and even the motives of Judith and Bon remain a mystery.

The narrators are uncertain as to whether love entered the relationship at all. While Mr. Compson states on numerous occasions that Judith and Bon did love each other, at other times he contradicts himself completely. About Bon he makes a number of damaging statements: that he loved Henry best; that his letters to Judith were "flowery," "insincere," and "tediously contrived;" that Bon was an "intending bigamist" and possibly a "blackguard"; that he had replaced the photograph of Judith with one of the octoroon and child. As for Judith, Mr. Compson believes that she was too much like Sutpen to love anyone at all. Along with Rosa and Quentin, he notes Judith's strange comportment when her fiance was

killed—her calm, impenetrable, frozen face—which Rosa, at least, interprets as evidence of the absence of grief. This apparent lack of emotion,
however, is more likely to be an indication of the depth of her feeling, the
coldness and the numbness revealing the severity of the blow she has
suffered.[2] Certainly, those tears which are shed on Bon's grave—the
weeping of the octoroon in that carefully staged show of grief—are unconvincing. Quentin and Shreve appear as little able as Mr. Compson to
reach any conclusion concerning the pair, Quentin protesting repeatedly
that this is not a love story and Shreve insisting that it is. Shreve's argu-
ments, however, are undeniably weak, particularly his sentimental theory
to explain Bon's replacement of Judith's picture with that of the octoroon
and child, his conjecture that it was Bon's way of saying to his sister,
" '*I was no good; do not grieve for me.*' "[3]

Shreve also raises the possibility that Bon is attracted to incest as a
means of stopping time. Perhaps Bon sees incest as a means of giving
permanence to the relationship, even if it means that "the vain evanesc-
ence of the fleshly encounter" will be translated into an eternity of damnation; as Shreve puts it, "maybe if there were sin too maybe you would
not be permitted to escape, uncouple, return" (*AA*, 323, 324). Such a
theory, of course, very much agrees with Quentin's own perspective in
The Sound and the Fury, and it is remarkable indeed that Shreve, and not
Quentin, is the one to offer it here.

Most of Bon's motives, however, are inextricably entangled with the
reasons that impell him toward miscegenation. At first glance, incest and
miscegenation appear to have little in common, the one indicating the
attraction of like to like and the other, a union of opposites. The two
coincide though in a number of areas, and in cases like that of Judith and
Bon where one relationship is superimposed on the other, these areas are
understandably strengthened and fortified.

One motive that appears commonly in both incest and miscegenation
is the desire for revenge. It is found certainly in most of the incestuous
relationships in Faulkner's works—figuring prominently, as we have noted,
in Jason's attraction to his niece and in Jewel's love for Addie. It seems
to be the primary impulse in Drusilla Hawk's efforts in *The Unvanquished*
to compromise her step-son.[4] In the garden scene at twilight where she
first tempts Bayard, Drusilla is impelled by a desire for revenge against
her husband, John Sartoris, an impulse prompted not so much by his
undisguised indifference to her as by his intention to be finished with the
killing of men. In the second temptation scene, that of Bayard's homecoming after his father's death, Drusilla's anger is aimed not at her husband but at his foes. On this occasion as before, however, it is really the
Southern code of violence that Drusilla defends. As she proffers the two

duelling pistols, Drusilla exhorts Bayard "in a voice fainting and passionate with promise" to assume the role of avenger:

> "Take them. I have kept them for you. I give them to you. Oh you will thank me, you
> will remember me who put into your hands what they say is an attribute only of God's,
> who took what belongs to heaven and gave it to you. Do you feel them? the long true
> barrels true as justice, the triggers (you have fired them) quick as retribution, the two
> of them slender and invincible and fatal as the physical shape of love?"[5]

Like that first snake in the garden, Drusilla offers not only the promise
of divinity that precipitated the Fall but also the carnal knowledge that
was the seal of the first sin.

Revenge is also a prominent element in literature's treatment of the
miscegenous relationship, the mulatto functioning here as the instrument
of the black man's revenge.[6] Just such an avenger is Charles Bon, whose
determination to marry his sister is motivated largely by a wish to make
his father pay in kind for the suffering inflicted on his mother and himself
because of their black blood. Miscegenation is also a vehicle for revenge
in "Elly," although here the roles are reversed, and the white partner, a
girl, is the one bent on vengeance; in this short story, which very much
resembles *Absalom*, Elly involves herself with a man believed to be part-
black in order to punish and eventually to destroy a grandmother she
hates.[7]

The black man's desire for vengeance is understandable in view of
the injustices of the Southern system, injustices that find in miscegenation
their perfect symbol. This relationship, in which a white man is allowed
to take a black woman who is not free to resist him, points to the exploitation of an entire people by "the white man's 'lust' for wealth and
power."[8] Nor is the black woman the only one made to suffer in such a
system; the white Southern woman becomes a victim too.[9] It is perhaps
this double victimization that Rosa has in mind when she describes a brief
moment of identification with Clytie in which the two of them are joined
by Clytie's arm on hers; it holds them "like a fierce umbilical cord, twin
sistered to the fell darkness which had produced her" (*AA*, 140). In the
miscegenous relationship of Bon and Judith, however, the usual situation
is reversed in that the white person is exploited by the black, although it
is still the woman who is abused. This reversal, however, only adds to
Bon's exploitation of Judith, evident already in his use of her to wreak
his vengeance on his father. Flying in the face of a system which makes
the black woman eminently available to the white man while the white
woman remains absolutely inaccessible to the black man, Bon's courtship
of Judith, if the facts were known, would destroy her.[10] Bon's willingness

to do this, however, is made eminently clear in his statement to Henry, a declaration he phrases as offensively as he can:

> — *No I'm not* [your brother]. *I'm the nigger that's going to sleep with your sister. Unless you stop me, Henry.* (AA, 358)

In *Go Down, Moses,* also, the element of exploitation is intensified in those relationships that are incestuous and miscegenous both. Particularly horrifying is old Carothers McCaslin's incest with his mulatto daughter, the twenty-three-year-old Tomasina—an affair that probably meant little more to him than "an afternoon's or a night's spittoon" (*GDM,* 270). This wrong, moreover, is repeated 106 years later when Roth Edmonds, a descendant of McCaslin who resembles him physically, takes as his mistress Tomasina's granddaughter, twice removed. While he also regards the mulatto woman as fair game for his sport, likening the pursuit of her to the hunting of coons and does, Roth Edmonds does evince some feelings of guilt and self-blame. In this there are small signs for hope.

In their guesswork on Bon's motives, though, Shreve and Bon return most persistently to the idea that Bon is drawn to Sutpen's Hundred by the desire for some kind of acknowledgment from Sutpen. The threat of incest is the instrument for wresting from Sutpen the recognition withdrawn because of the black blood. Sutpen's refusal to provide this sign of recognition, however, repeats his own rejection, as a youth, at the plantation door and ensures the perpetuation of a dismal cycle of repudiation continuing through Bon, Charles Etienne, and Jim Bond. A similar pattern of rejection intertwined with themes of incest and miscegenation is found in *Go Down, Moses*: Carothers McCaslin's attempt to buy off his mulatto son-grandson with a bequest in a will; and five generations later, Roth Edmonds' repetition of this evasion of responsibility with an envelope of banknotes.[11]

In miscegenation it is the absence of the father that is most acutely felt; in incest, as we have noted, the loss or defection of the mother has the greatest effect. In both relationships the problem of self-definition, not surprisingly, is a prominent one. The incestuous partner's uneasiness as to who he may be is evident in his rejection of the world outside and in his adherence to someone he perceives as an image of himself. In miscegenation several forms of identity crisis are involved: the black partner suffers the rootlessness of the person wrenched from his homeland; the white partner fears that the relationship will cost him his identity— an absorption of his white blood by the black. But it is the product of the union, the mulatto, who suffers most acutely: a person of mixed blood, he does not know what he is; fatherless, he does not know who he is.

The dilemma of the mulatto, however, provides a perfect metaphor for the brotherhood of man; becuse he could be the brother of anyone, he must be considered the kinsman of all. As a child, Bon felt that it must be for everyone as it was for him, "all boy flesh that walked and breathed stemming from that one ambiguous eluded dark fatherhead and so brothered perennial and ubiquitous everywhere under the sun—" (*AA*, 299).

The problems of self-definition in incest and miscegenation, already acute, are worsened by the role violations both relationships incur. A daughter may be compelled to double as her father's mistress or "wife," like Tomasina of *Go Down, Moses*, "that one that was its own mother too"; while the child of such a union, like Tomey's Turl, becomes a son to his grandfather and the offspring of his sister (*GDM*, 362).[12] Similarly, the mulatto, carrying in his veins the blood of master and slave, conquered and conqueror, is torn in two opposing directions. Clytie is the "agent" of her own "crucifixion"; Sam Fathers is "himself his own battleground, the scene of his own vanquishment and the mausoleum of his defeat" (*GDM*, 168). The particular horror, however, of miscegenation in the Old South was the fact that mulatto offspring were property and could be bought and sold by the white father/master. Sam Fathers was "swapped" by his father for an "underbred" horse; Charles Etienne is the "complete chattel of him who, begetting him, owned him body and soul to sell (if he chose) like a calf or puppy or sheep" (*AA*, 114).

Another prominent Faulknerian theme that links incest and miscegenation, in opposition to one another however, is the emotions' repression and revenge. In relations that fall short of actual incest, as most of the incestuous relationships in Faulkner do, repression is practiced. In the miscegenation, however, all restraints are abandoned, an unfettering that derives largely from the white partner's perception of the black as a primitive, as the personification of life's dark desires. Such a view is clearly held by Mr. Compson, who sees the black blood of Bon's octoroon mistress as the conduit of all sexual desire. And in *Light in August* this attitude is demonstrated also by Joanna Burden when she addresses Joe Christmas in moments of passion as "Negro! Negro! Negro!" (*LA*, 245).[13] Joanna's story, in fact, provides a beautiful example of the revenge of repressed emotions; it presents a woman who preserves her "purity" for some forty-odd years and then flings herself into the bizarre and frenzied eroticism of an affair with a part-black man.

The conjunction of incest and miscegenation in Judith's and Bon's relationship, then, strengthens the causes that lead Bon to Judith, and it also intensifies and fortifies those qualities that are common to both relationships. The merging of the two themes serves yet another purpose: to provide a means by which the racial prejudices of the Southerner can be properly exposed, the incest serving as a yardstick with which to measure the extent of the South's blindness.[14] Henry's inability to swallow the miscegenation in the marriage, although he has managed to stomach the incest, an act that comes under a near-universal taboo and is considered inimical to civilization itself—this constitutes, surely, a powerful comment on the Southerner's rejection of his black brother.[15]

Henry, however, does not find it easy to accept even the incest, which he must somehow reconcile with his Methodist morals. For this reason, to justify the unjustifiable, he turns to history and the examples it affords. Henry argues that others have committed this sin and apparently suffered no harm, citing in particular a John of Lorraine:

> " 'But kings have done it! Even dukes! There was that Lorraine duke named John something that married his sister. The Pope excommunicated him but it didn't hurt! It didn't hurt! They were still husband and wife. They were still alive. They still loved!' " (*AA*, 342)

The duke that Henry probably has in mind here, for history contains no record of a Duke John of Lorraine, is Lothar II, a ninth-century king of that country.[16] He would certainly have been an obvious candidate on whom to light, for he belonged to a family notorious for its incestuous entanglements. One such entanglement, an international cause célèbre that "occupied all christendom nearly fifteen years," centered on Lothar's efforts to extricate himself from a childless marriage. Seizing the only weapon at hand in his attempt to obtain a divorce, Lothar repeatedly accused his wife, Theutberga, of committing incest with her brother. These charges, however, left the church unmoved; instead of granting a divorce, it excommunicated Lothar's mistress, Waldrada, and threatened to place Lothar and Theutberga under the ban too. In the course of the controversy, Theutberga appealed to Charles the Bald, Lothar's uncle and the king of France, who later succeeded his nephew to the throne of Lorraine. In reprisal against Charles for befriending his wife, Lothar then took under his protection Charles' daughter Judith, the queen of Wessex whose marriage to her step-son had shocked all England. Matters were further complicated for Charles when his two sons mounted against him a serious revolt, one in which the younger son Charles, who had married earlier without his father's blessing, proved particularly troublesome. The unfortunate Charles, however, died at an early age, "weakened in his intellectual faculties" by a blow to the head.[17]

In the history of these Carolingian kings there begin to emerge certain very familiar features: the brother-sister incest in Lothar's story, his desperate efforts to establish a dynasty, the threat of excommunication and the lowering of the ban, the name of Charles the Bald, the French connection of this king, the revolt of his two sons, the incestuous marriage of his daughter, the daughter's name of Judith, the forbidden marriage of Charles and his untimely death, and finally the mental impairment of Charles the Bald's heir.[18] While this history is only roughly analogous to the Sutpen chronicle, the similarities suggest that Lothar may have served as a source for Henry's duke or perhaps that Charles the Bald was a model for Sutpen. It is a possibility that is strengthened, certainly, by the fact that Lothar's story was not unknown to Faulkner. In *Knight's Gambit* the names Judith and Lothar both appear in Charles Mallison's reference to his grandmother's books—"the somber tomes through which moved . . . the men and women who were to christian-name a whole generation: the Clarissas and Judiths and Marguerites, the St. Elmos, and Rolands and Lothairs."[19] Lothar is mentioned also in the Foreword of *The Faulkner Reader,* where Faulkner characterized the 1880's and 1890's as "that time when women did most of the book-buying and reading too, naming their children Byron and Clarissa and St. Elmo and Lothair. . . ."[20] Two lines later in the Foreword there appears a reference to a King John of Poland who may, perhaps, have lent his name to Henry's duke of Lorraine. It is worth noting, at any rate, that the two names which Faulkner gave to Sutpen, before settling on Thomas, were Charles and John.[21]

Henry, however, fails in his recourse to history to justify incest. First, he undercuts his own argument with a statement to the effect that the past is irrelevant, powerless, immaterial:

> " 'But that Lorraine duke did it! There must have been lots in the world who have done it that people dont know about, that maybe they suffered for it and died for it and are in hell now for it. But they did it and it dont matter now; even the ones we do know about are just names now and it dont matter now.' " (*AA*, 343)

This argument, however, is clearly untenable. The point it tries to make is contrary to the statement that the book itself is making, that history does matter, that the past is never dead and forgotten. Secondly, as Henry points out later, it is not the pope's or the duke's or Bon's Hell—that is, an easy, tolerant Catholic Hell—in which Sutpen and his three progeny will find themselves but in "the everlasting damnation" of the Southern Methodist Church. The most important reason, however, for Henry's failure to justify incest with his duke of Lorraine is the fact that the lessons of history simply do not support his position; the chronicles of these Carolingian kings, like the Sutpen story itself, teach us that incest—and even the threat, suggestion, or charge of incest—destroys families and wrecks kingdoms. Ultimately, of course, kings and dukes have little to do with Henry's decision to countenance the incest; it is his love for Bon which finally overrides both his "heredity" and his "training."[22]

A second incestuous relationship in the triangle of Sutpen offspring is that of Judith and Henry. According to Mr. Compson, it is an extraordinary relationship: "curious and unusual," "closer than the traditional loyalty of brother and sister even," a case of a "single personality with two bodies" (*AA*, 79, 91–92, 100). Like Darl and Dewey Dell (or Satan and Sin), Judith and Henry enjoy special powers of communication: as children they anticipated "one another's actions as two birds leave a limb at the same instant" (*AA*, 99); later that same "telepathy" explains Henry's ability to win Judith for Bon, despite the forty miles separating Oxford and Jefferson. For it is Henry, not Bon, who seduces Judith, seducing "her to his own vicarious image which walked and breathed with Bon's body" (*AA*, 107). Had Bon been unrelated by blood to Judith, as Mr. Compson thought him to be, then Henry's relationship with his sister would truly have been "the pure and perfect incest" (*AA*, 96).[23]

Like the relationships of Caddy and Quentin, Narcissa and Horace, the "incest" of Judith and Henry reveals the attraction of opposites. Judith is the Sutpen—strong, ruthless, and bold, taking what she wants and willing to kill, if she must, to get it; Henry is the Coldfield "with the Coldfield cluttering of morality and rules of right and wrong" (*AA*, 120). The one occasion on which Henry resembles Judith is the confrontation between the two in Judith's bedroom at Sutpen's Hundred; in telling his sister he has just killed Bon, Henry plays for once the part of a Sutpen. What follows, however, simply confirms the essential differences between the two: Henry escapes into exile, remains away for years, and then returns a frail old man waiting to die; while Judith, remaining behind to pick up the pieces, assumes the burden of responsibility not only for her own life but for Clytie's and Charles Etienne's as well. The sister strong and the brother weak, the Sutpen siblings are obverse images of one another, opposing halves of the "single personality" of which Mr. Compson speaks. Like Caddy and Quentin and Narcissa and Horace, they point to the fall from some original wholeness. This opposition of Coldfield and Sutpen may also indicate, however, the effort to recover that wholeness through incest, through the repetition in the next generation of the pairing of their parents.

Like other sibling couples in Faulkner—the Compsons, the Bundrens, and the Benbows, Judith and Henry lack a true mother, a deprivation that contributes greatly to the likelihood of incest occurring.[24] Like these other mothers who have retreated for one reason or another—death, illness, deficiencies of character—Ellen Coldfield is not present to her children. A shallow and superficial woman suffering from delusions of grandeur, she escapes "into a world of pure illusion in which, safe from any harm, she moved, lived, from attitude to attitude" (*AA*, 69). When this bubble bursts, she retreats even further, retiring to her "darkened room," where she takes to her bed and waits for death; it is the Coldfield way, a solution embraced also by her father and later by her son. An even worse mother than the vacuous Ellen, more distant and less loving, is Eulalia Bon, who also lives in a world of her own, a place where hatred is the only reality and where her son figures chiefly as the instrument of her revenge. There are, additionally, two other mothers in *Absalom* who are removed from their children: Rosa's is lost to her at birth, and Sutpen's dies when he is ten.

The isolation that usually characterizes the incestuous family in Faulkner and in clinical studies, too, is found also in the life at Sutpen's Hundred. Henry and Judith lead remote and lonely lives; they are like two people "marooned at birth on a desert island: the island here Sutpen's Hundred; the solitude, the shadow of that father" whom neither the town nor even the Coldfields could bring themselves to accept and assimilate (*AA*, 99). Even the house at Sutpen's Hundred possesses an aversion to people, "an incontrovertible affirmation for emptiness, desertion; an insurmountable resistance to occupancy . . . save by the ruthless and the strong" (*AA*, 85). As in actual cases of incest, where the isolation that encouraged the act is itself intensified by what it had promoted, in the Sutpens' story, too, life becomes increasingly desolate. Following the murder of Bon, the climactic conclusion to the Sutpens' three-sided "incest," Henry vanishes; Judith, alone save for Clytie and for a time Bon's son, remains behind at Sutpen's Hundred—possessed of no friends, paying no calls, avoiding the town.

But incest is present in *Absalom* not only in the Sutpen family but also in narrator Quentin Compson's consciousness of his own incestuous feelings. This is particularly evident at that point of the story where he balks at the door he cannot pass: that scene in Judith's bedroom when Henry confronts his sister with the news of Bon's death. It is a scene that strongly implies, at least in Quentin's visualization of the event, that Henry's reason for killing Bon has not been the prevention of incest or even miscegenation but the appeasement of his own jealous love. There is, first of all, a certain suggestiveness in the placement of the scene in Judith's bedroom and in the deshabille of the half-clad girl, clutching the wedding gown hastily before her. More significant, however, are Henry's first words to his sister as he bursts through the door, stating immediately what is foremost in his mind, his reason for killing Bon: *"Now you cant marry him"* (*AA*, 172). This pronouncement, in which the notes of revenge are

mixed undeniably with those of triumph, makes no mention of Bon's kinship or his black blood but offers as reason instead the simple fact of her
marrying another man. Also important to this scene is the image of the
door, which seems to have the same sexual connotations here that it holds
in *Soldier's Pay*; there Faulkner states that sex and death are "the front
door and the back door of the world," an association that he may well
have obtained from *The Golden Bough* (*SP,* 295).[25] The door that Henry
"crashed," however, is one that Quentin, quite literally, cannot "pass."
At the book's close, he cannot bring himself, despite the importunings of
Rosa, to break down the door at Sutpen's Hundred and must slip into the
house by way of the window.[26] Nor is Quentin able to pass the door in a
figurative sense; he cannot act as Henry could, cannot confront and defeat
his sister's suitor.

The third side of the Sutpen triangle consists of the relationship of
Henry and Bon, a complex affair containing elements not only of incest
and miscegenation but homosexuality as well. In his narrative, which
places the relationship under the closest scrutiny, Mr. Compson makes
quite clear the nature of Henry's and Bon's affection—its affinity with
Greek love.[27] Henry feels for his brother "that complete and abnegant
devotion which only a youth, never a woman, gives to another youth or
a man" (*AA,* 107). And Bon loves Henry more than he loves Judith; she
is the "shadow" of the brother through whom "he will consummate the
love whose actual object was the youth" (*AA,* 108). But the incestuous
theme is not ignored in this relationship; it is, in fact, curiously entangled
and entwined with the homosexual interest. As in many case studies,
where it appears that one relationship breeds the other, in the Sutpen
story also the two relationships seem to feed and nourish one another in
a strange sort of reciprocity; the homosexuality of the brothers serves as
a means of attaining incest with the sister, and the incest in turn provides
a way of satisfying the homoerotic desires.[28] The superimposing of one
theme upon the other in the brothers' relationship points also to the syn-
onymity of the two in a number of regards. Each is a forbidden relationship, prohibited by law; each constitutes a violation of the rules of nature,
of fertility and propogation; and each represents a distortion of brotherly
love.

It would be difficult, however, to find two brothers less alike than
Henry and Bon, a dissimilarity which points again to the function of
incestuous partners as mirror images of one another. Henry is the asser-
tive man of action, impulsive and volatile, living by instinct rather than
reason; Bon is the spectator—passive, indolent, detached, cerebral.[29]
Henry is the country provincial, accustomed to rough play and crude
pleasures; Bon, the urban sophisticate—elegant, experienced, polished,

refined. The younger brother descends from the Anglo-Saxon Puritan tradition and its grim, stern, and humorless perspective; the elder is heir to Roman Catholicism's Latin culture—sensuous, opulent, richly ornate. It is a polarization which suggests the conflict or conjunction of the New World and the Old, of the native and the alien—those strains that meet also in the South's culture to create what has sometimes been observed as the split in the Southern psyche.[30]

A prime ingredient in the relationship of Henry and Bon is exploitation, an element that admittedly characterizes almost every relationship in the novel. Henry exploits Bon, whom he uses as a vehicle for the vicarious seduction of Judith; and Bon, in his courtship of Judith, manipulates his brother "with cold and cat-like inscrutable calculation" (AA, 110).[31] Both Henry and Bon exploit also the sister, whom they regard as an avenue to one another. Additionally, Mr. Compson suggests that Bon may be attracted by neither Henry nor Judith, but by the life itself at Sutpen's Hundred, and hence may be manipulating both the Sutpen siblings at once.

The exploitive and manipulative character of the relationship, however, cannot account for its culmination in fratricide. Why the Sutpens' incestuous triangle should erupt in such a fashion is, in fact, the central and compelling problem of the novel, one which none of the narrators is able to answer with complete satisfaction.[32] Rosa Coldfield reaches no conclusion; and Mr. Compson is finally stumped also, although he saddles Bon with much of the blame, stressing Henry's love, grief, devotion to principle, and readiness to sacrifice as opposed to what he sees as Bon's intransigence, not unlike Sutpen's own. Quentin and Shreve suggest that it is the prevention first of incest and then of miscegenation, Quentin also presenting in his oblique fashion the possibility that it is Henry's jealous love for Judith.[33] If the conjecturing provides no ready answers, however, it makes the problem clear—that Henry's and Bon's relationship is an incredibly complex affair, involving as it does incest, homosexuality, miscegenation, and fratricide. All of these elements, though, do point in one direction: the exploitation, perversion, and, finally, the rejection of brotherly love.

Another Faulkner character who tries, without success however, to kill his sister's Latin lover, is Max Harriss of "Knight's Gambit," a story which comes close to being an Absalom in modern setting. The two works, certainly, share a significant number of features: the triad of brother, sister, and Latin lover; the overtones of incest in the sibling relationship; the brother's attempt on the lover's life; the close physical resemblance of brother and sister; the isolation of the family and its alienation from the community; the cold and ruthless character of the father; the unfolding of the drama against the backdrop of a bloody war. In each work, also, the incest serves to reveal and reflect what is worst in the culture, whether it is the interiority and defensiveness of the Old South or the solipsism and self-absorption of the New. There is no question in "Knight's Gambit," however, concerning the brother's motives. A vicious young man who is unaccustomed to being thwarted, Max tries to kill Sebastian Gualdres because of his fear and despair at the thought of losing his sister.

In *Absalom, Absalom!*, the theme of incest appears also in the relationship of Thomas Sutpen and his sister-in-law, Rosa. Since, however, the couple are related by the ties of affinity rather than blood, the issue is not as clearly drawn as in the case of the Sutpen siblings. In 1865 their marriage would not have been illegal, but biblical law and earlier church laws would have prohibited as incestuous any match between them.[34] The word incest is never attached to the pair and their projected marriage, but we are made aware in subtle ways that this would be a forbidden match. An air of secrecy and furtiveness hangs over the engagement, and it leads not to marriage but to shame and outrage. And we never lose sight of the fact that Rosa is betrothed to her sister's husband. Rosa reminds us as she rants against Milly Jones, Wash's "*granddaughter who was to supplant me, if not in my sister's house at least in my sister's bed*" (*AA*, 134). When Sutpen gives Rosa a ring to seal their engagement, it is Ellen's wedding ring that he places on her finger. Mr. Compson in particular draws attention to the role violations in such a relationship when he observes that, had Judith and Bon married, Rosa "would have lived in her dead sister's family only as the aunt which she actually was" (*AA*, 67–68). In a similar case in *The Unvanquished*, where the couple are related also by the bonds of affinity and marry in spite of it, the ambiguity of Drusilla's and John's relationship is stressed by Aunt Louisa's admonishment of her daughter, " 'At least don't call him *Cousin* John where strangers can hear you' " (*Uv*, 220).

The courtship of Sutpen and Rosa, moreover, resembles in many respects the relationships of Faulkner's more clearly incestuous couples. These two, for instance, like the others, lead very solitary lives. Losing her mother at birth and hating her father for that loss, Rosa is a person who never knows love, not even that parental affection "*which is the meed and due of all mammalian meat*" (*AA*, 146). She follows an essentially vicarious existence, eavesdropping as a child at "closed forbidden doors" and falling heir later to Ellen's husband as she had inherited her clothes. The greater part of her life, the forty-three years of "static outrage" into which she is thrust by Sutpen's indelicate proposal, is spent cloistered in the "impregnable solitude" of her grim little house. In his youth, Sutpen too knows what it is to be shut out by a closed door, an experience he finds so painful that it casts its shadow over the whole of his existence and determines the course of his life. As a man, Sutpen dwells apart from, and often opposed to, the community of men; friendless save for General Compson, he is loved by no one, and he trusts nobody. Even the fellowship of the family he rejects, refusing to share, even once, in the communion of the Sunday meal at the Coldfield's house.

The repression of the instincts and their subsequent revenge, a theme linked often with incest in Faulkner, figures also in the relationship of Sutpen and Rosa. It is associated primarily with Rosa, a "child-like," "doll-sized" woman, who reveals in her stunted physical frame the dwarfing of her emotional life. In a sense, Rosa never enters life at all but remains unborn, *"overdue because of some caesarean lack"* (*AA*, 144). While she does not know fulfillment, though, Rosa is no stranger to desire; like a plant bereft of bloom and leaf, she is still possessed of *"root and urge,"* her inheritance *"too from all the unsistered Eves since the Snake"* (*AA*, 144). And as the highly suggestive—even erotic—imagery of her rhetoric suggests, Rosa never roots these instincts from their soil; it is, however, bitter fruit that they now yield: hate, frustration, and the thirst for revenge. Such a harvest is reaped also in *The Unvanquished* by Drusilla, whose rigidly repressed emotions emerge in a particularly virulent form—her passionate espousal of the Southern code of vengeance.[35]

It is the element of exploitation, however, which is the salient feature of Rosa's and Sutpen's abortive courtship. A man who generally tolerates people only insofar as they are useful to him, Sutpen pursues Rosa with just one goal in mind: a son and heir. It is a purpose which is made abundantly clear to Rosa when Sutpen suggests that a trial breeding should preface the marriage, that she should first produce a son and then become his wife—Sutpen speaking *"the bald outrageous words exactly as if he were consulting with Jones or with some other man about a bitch dog or a cow or mare"* (*AA*, 168). Sutpen's image in this affair is not improved, moreover, by Rosa's depiction of herself as the innocent victim, a naive young girl who sacrifices all dreams of romance to marry a fifty-nine-year-old "mad man" who does not love her but needs her.[36] A somewhat similar relationship appears in *Pylon* in the seduction of the fifteen-year-old Laverne by her older sister's husband, a man in the neighborhood of twenty-seven or twenty-nine. Here the exploitation of the girl is made quite plain. It is a tawdry affair, one that consists, for Laverne, of "being wallowed around in the back seat of a car" after a few sodas and dances in a back alley "dive"; and its ugliness is increased by unhappy scenes with the sister, confrontations in which the unpleasantness of lies and deceit is compounded by her lover's betrayals of her "to save his own face."[37]

Rosa's and Sutpen's courtship also resembles other incestuous relationships in Faulkner's works, particularly that of Caddy and Quentin, in
Sutpen's attraction to incest as a means of halting time. While Quentin,
however, hopes to move beyond historical time, to restore Caddy's lost
innocence and return to Eden, Sutpen entertains less exalted ambitions;
he merely wants to turn back the clock so that he can "catch up." Nearing
sixty and desperately aware of the shortness of time in which to rebuild
his empire and re-establish his dynasty, Sutpen sees marriage to Rosa as
a way to recover not only the wife and the son but also the time he has
lost. Rosa tells us that, on the occasion of their engagement, it seemed
"as though in the restoration of that ring to a living finger he had turned
all time back twenty years and stopped it, froze it" (AA, 165). Additionally, Sutpen hopes the sons that will issue from this union will be his
"bulwark" against time, his assurance of the immortality his soul craves.
While the courtship of Rosa ultimately fails Sutpen in his efforts to halt
time, this ill-starred romance does have that unexpected and undesired
effect for Rosa. Sutpen's great "insult," his suggestion that "they breed
for test and sample," stops her dead in her tracks and leaves her for the
next forty-three years arrested in an attitude of impotent outrage (AA,
177). When she does in fact die, Miss Rosa appropriately is laid to rest
in frozen earth; the one brief sign of life in that cold scene is the redworm
in the clod of earth, recalling the "one red instant's fierce obliteration"
of "shibboleth" in Rosa's life, her brief surrender to Sutpen.[38] In much
the same way, the South, "dead since 1865 and peopled with garrulous
outraged baffled ghosts," is arrested in its attitudes by the great catastrophe of the Civil War (AA, 9).

But incest satisfies Sutpen's dynastic ambitions no better than it met
the demands of England's Henry VIII, a man who wanted sons as desperately and who may, in fact, have served as a source for Sutpen.[39] Such
a kingly model is suggested, certainly, in the many references to the mo-
narchical existence at Sutpen's Hundred: the house is a "baronial splen-
dor" and Sutpen's Hundred a "king's grant"; Bon's liaison with the
octoroon is a "morganatic" marriage, Judith a "prolific queen," Wash a
"retainer" to Sutpen the "baron"; the realization of Sutpen's dream is
the "coronation" of his ambition, and Sutpen himself is a man who has
"put aside his first wife like eleventh-and twelfth-century kings did" (AA,
240). And Sutpen resembles Henry in many ways. They are similar physically, both men possessing large frames, pale eyes, and short reddish
beards. In character and personality the two are also compatible. Like
Henry, Sutpen rejects his friends and abandons his "wives." His contempt
for women rivals even Henry's, his designation of Milly as a "mare"
echoing the king's own reference to Anne of Cleaves as "the Flanders

mare."[40] Sutpen's peculiar innocence is akin to the morality of Henry, who "more than most . . . found it difficult to distinguish between what was right and what he desired."[41] Additionally, Sutpen's daughter, Judith, is not unlike Henry's successor, Elizabeth, a woman known for her cool humanism, independence, and intelligence.

Sutpen's story, too, echoes that of Henry in many respects. Henry and Sutpen both fathered sons who were not in legitimate line and who met with untimely deaths. Both men married at an early age, taking as their wives women of Spanish extraction, whom they later discarded because of their inability to provide acceptable heirs. Each of these wives, in her battles with her husband, enlisted the aid of a kinsman named Charles, Eulalia relying on her son and Catherine turning to her nephew, Emperor Charles V. In divorcing their first wives and taking new spouses, both men in effect rejected the Catholic Church and allied themselves with Puritanism and the Protestant faith, an alliance which was an uneasy one, however, for both Henry and Sutpen, who found themselves often at odds with the church. The wives or mistresses of these men frequently met with unhappy ends; like two of Henry's wives, Milly Jones lost her head (or very nearly was beheaded), and the image of the slashed throat is associated also with Ellen. Additionally, over the lives of both Henry and Sutpen lay the shadow of a great civil war: the Wars between the Roses and the American Civil War.

Most important for our purposes, however, is the part that incest plays in these stories, its role in thwarting the dynastic ambitions of these men. Sutpen's grandiose scheme to create a latter-day dukedom collapses twice under the threat of incest in the family—first when two of his children decide to marry and, secondly, when he determines to take his sister-in-law as a wife. Henry contracted three marriages that could be considered incestuous: his marriage to Catherine of Aragon, widow of his brother, Arthur; to Anne Boleyn—a woman who was rumored to be his natural daughter, who was in fact the sister of his mistress, and who was convicted of incest with her brother George; and to Jane Seymour, who was related to him within the fourth degree of consanguinity. These marriages did not establish his line; they produced two daughters, Mary and Elizabeth, and a son who died at sixteen, surviving his father by just six years. If the marriages seem to us not clearly incestuous and if the incest seems to us unconnected to the dearth of sons, this interpretation was not shared by Henry, who employed the charge of incest repeatedly to divest himself of his barren (or sonless) wives. The uses to which incest had been put in the past in suits for royal annulments were, of course, well known to Henry, who was a collateral descendant of Lothar II.[42]

If Faulkner did indeed employ Henry VIII as a source for Sutpen, his recourse to history for a model is not surprising. Faulkner was a student of the past, and his "novels are drenched in history."[43] Furthermore, of all the books in the canon, *Absalom, Absalom!* is the most historical, concerning itself not only with history and with the South's consciousness of its past but also with historiography, the process of recording that past. Nor is it surprising that the historical figure Faulkner should choose is Henry; his selection of a man notorious for his involvement with incest is but one more instance of the importance which attaches to the incest theme in Faulkner.

More obvious, however, is the debt that Sutpen's portrait owes to that of Milton's Satan. Sutpen is undoubtedly one of Faulkner's most diabolical characters, and nowhere is this legacy more evident than in the matter of pride. In her obsessive analysis of Sutpen, Rosa quite correctly singles out this quality for special condemnation: *"I see the analogy myself now: the accelerating circle's fatal curving course of his ruthless pride, his lust for vain magnificence, though I did not then"* (*AA*, 162). This pride is all of a piece with the hubris of Satan, that arrogance which he displays so baldly in the address to the angels of the North:

> We know no time when we were not as now;
> Know none before us, self-begot, self-rais'd
> By our own quick'ning power, when fatal course
> Had circl'd his full Orb, the birth mature
> Of this our native Heav'n, Ethereal Sons. (*PL* V.859–63)

Like the diabolical Jason, Sutpen is guilty also of a satanic envy, a quality that is best relayed, in *Absalom* as in *The Sound and the Fury,* by the imagery of the thicket; the thicket in Faulkner, we recall, functions much as the brambles circling Milton's Paradise, pointing like them to the longing and envy of the outsider looking in. As a boy, Sutpen hides in the "tangled shrubbery" of the plantation lawn to watch the planter swinging in his hammock, fanned by a slave. Years later, when an old and battered Sutpen realizes that perhaps Rosa can replenish his house with sons, he sees in her "the absence of black morass and snarled vine and creeper"— not the promise of Paradise but an escape, certainly, from Hell (*AA*, 166).

Above all, Sutpen is ambitious, and it is most fitting that his portrait should draw on that particular avatar of Satan who was the world's first tyrant: Nimrod, the empire-builder.[44] Like Nimrod, who marches west from Eden into the plain, Sutpen moves westward from an Edenic mountain homeland. Intent on "getting a name for themselves," Nimrod and his "crew" construct, from brick and "a black bituminous gurge" that "Boils out from under ground," an edifice that challenges Heaven itself:

the Tower of Babel (*PL* XII.41–42). Spurred also by the desire for recognition (he will marry Ellen for the Coldfield name), Sutpen erects the enormous brick mansion at Sutpen's Hundred. It is a visible monument to that ambition which Faulkner calls innocence; it emerges from the black mire of the swamp in much the same manner that Sutpen's innocence, following the traumatic rejection at the plantation door, seems to rise "like a monument" from "a limitless flat plain" (*AA*, 238). Again like Nimrod, a hunter who makes "Men not Beasts . . . his game," Sutpen undertakes the subjugation of his fellow man (*PL* XII.30). The similarity is apparent particularly in the pitiless pursuit and capture of Sutpen's Hundred's escaped architect, an incident that illustrates not only the ruthlessness of Sutpen but also the dangers to others of trafficking with evil. Brought to earth finally, despite his efforts to engineer himself beyond the reach of Sutpen's hounds and slaves, the little Frenchman shares the fate of Milton's Mulciber, architect of that monument called Pandemonium: "nor did he scape / By all his Engines, but was headlong sent / With his industrious crew to build in hell" (*PL* I.749–51).[45] Finally, just as Nimrod's ambitions are thwarted when God visits his builders with "the jangling of tongues unknown," so does Sutpen's mansion, built by a "crew" of blacks "who could speak no English yet," in the end come tumbling down (*PL* XII.55; *AA*, 36).

The last gasp of Sutpen's ambitions, his effort to recover "the Sutpen's Hundred which he remembered and had lost," destroys him (*AA*, 184).[46] It is a measure born of desperation, as Quentin makes clear:

> *Mad impotent old man who . . . must have seen himself as the old wornout cannon which realizes that it can deliver just one more fierce shot and crumble to dust in its own furious blast and recoil.* (*AA*, 181)

And these machinations will explode in his face, just as Satan's evil "like a devilish Engine back recoils / Upon himself" (*PL* IV.17–18). The worst punishment for evil, however, is the evil itself; Satan suffers most from the inescapable knowledge of what he has become:

> horror and doubt distract
> His troubl'd thoughts, and from the bottom stir
> The Hell within him, for within him Hell
> He brings, and round about him, nor from Hell
> One step no more than from himself can fly
> By change of place. . . . (*PL*, IV.18–23)

While the innocent Sutpen never attains to Satan's self-knowledge, he too is entrapped in the Hell of his own wickedness, a condition suggested particularly in Rosa's evocation of his ghost—"Itself circumambient and enclosed by its effluvium of hell, its aura of unregeneration" (*AA,* 13).

Just as Satan, however, retains a vestigial "brightness," so Sutpen is not entirely blackened, revealing on occasion qualities we respect and admire. He has, unquestionably, great strength and courage, and he has about him a largeness and grandeur that dwarf by comparison all the narrators who attempt to tell his story. Like Satan completing his magnificent journey through Milton's "vast abrupt," Sutpen "would abrupt" into Jefferson: "Out of quiet thunderclap he would abrupt (man-horse-demon) upon a scene peaceful and decorous as a schoolprize water color, faint sulphur-reek still in hair clothes and beard" (*PL* II.409; *AA,* 8). It is an analogy strengthened by Sutpen's physical resemblance, on this occasion, to the bold fiend who escapes from Hell and "explores his solitary flight"; Sutpen "looked like a man who had been through a solitary furnace experience . . . like an explorer say" (*PL* II.632; *AA,* 32). The comparison is accurate, for Sutpen has left behind in Haiti a Hell of Miltonic proportions; details in Faulkner's description of the slave rebellion—the "smoke and smell of burning cane," the "glare" of the fire in the "throbbing darkness," the planter's and the girl's progress across the "burned land," the "desolate solitude," the metaphor of the volcano—evoke the inferno of *Paradise Lost*: the "stench and smoke," the "darkness visible," Satan's "uneasy steps / Over the burning marl," "the seat of desolation," its resemblance to a scene left by "thund'ring Aetna" (*AA,* 251–54; *PL* I.63, 181, 295, 320–37). Another of Sutpen's qualities that commands admiration is his remarkable determination, the "fierce constant will' that is a match for Satan's own "unconquerable Will." Not even the South's defeat can effect Sutpen's submission; when he returns to Sutpen's Hundred "to find that he had lost more than the war even, though not absolutely all," he displays the resoluteness of Satan declaring in Hell, "What though the field be lost? / All is not lost" (*AA,* 363; *PL* I. 105–106). Faced later with the eminent collapse of his dynasty, Sutpen remains "invincible and unafraid"; in a passage that summons the immensity and awesomeness of Satan in Book I, "Prone on the Flood, extended large and long," Rosa describes Sutpen's attempts to preserve his domain: He was *"diffused (not attenuated to thinness but enlarged, magnified encompassing as though in a prolonged and unbroken instant of tremendous effort embracing and holding intact that ten-mile square . . .)"* (*PL* I.195; *AA,* 162–63).

Even as the Miltonic echoes stress Sutpen's heroic stature, however, they also point to its fragility. Wash's idealization of Sutpen is expressed most extravagantly in his vision of the Colonel "galloping . . . forever and forever immortal beneath the brandished saber and the shot-torn flags rushing down a sky in color like thunder" (*AA*, 288); but this segment also recalls the one instant that Satan falters in his daring journey through space:

> all unawares
> Flutt'ring his pennons vain plumb down he drops
> Ten thousand fadom deep, and to this hour
> Down had been falling, had not by ill chance
> The strong rebuff of some tumultuous cloud
> Instinct with Fire and Nitre hurried him
> As many miles aloft. . . . (*PL* II.932–38)[47]

When Sutpen finally is cut down by Wash's scythe (or Milton's "Scythe of Time"), he ends, not in a godlike fall from grace, but tumbled in his coffin "into a ditch."[48]

As any good avatar of Satan, Sutpen generates Sin. One of these several types of Sin that emerge so clearly in *Absalom* is Clytie, the mulatto daughter that Sutpen has quite literally created. Clytie recalls Satan's offspring in a number of respects: her strong resemblance to her father, her role of Cerberean watchdog in her father's "private hell," the suggestion (mistaken however) that she has conceived a son by Sutpen.[49] Clytie's identification with the fallen angels is suggested, additionally, in Shreve's description of the old woman's diminishing physical frame: "her body just grew smaller and smaller like something being shrunk in a furnace, like the Bornese do their captured heads"; similarly, the fallen angels thronging into Pandemonium are transformed into "less than smallest Dwarfs . . . like that Pigmean Race Beyond the *Indian* Mount" (*AA*, 215; *PL* I.779–81). Clytie's kinship with Sin, however, points not to a wickedness in her, not to wrongs that she has committed but to those that she has endured, the exploitation that is symbolized by the pigment of her coffee-colored skin. When Rosa defines her as "*amoral evil's undeviating absolute*," she imputes to Clytie an evil that is not her own (*AA*, 138).

Two other types of Sin generated by Sutpen, in the sense that he makes them what they become, are Eulalia and Rosa. Eulalia's identification with the fallen angels and with the "Snaky Sorceress" Sin is most evident in a scene in New Orleans with her lawyer; her reptilian nature suggested by the rope-like strands of her "lank iron-colored hair" and the dress that resembles "a section of limp stove pipe," Eulalia clutches the lawyer's forged letter "as if she knew she would have only a second to read it in," a second before her eyes touched it, and it "took fire," "leaving . . . a black crumbling blank carbon ash in her hand" (*AA*, 304–5). This scene recalls the fallen angels' transformation into serpents in Book X;

clustered in fruit-laden trees "thicker than the snaky locks / That curl'd Megaera," they attempted to assuage their unbearable hunger and thirst but "instead of Fruit / Chew'd bitter Ashes" (*PL* X.559–65).[50] Re-enacting the original sin like Satan's crew, the vindictive Eulalia can expect a similar reward. The most malevolent woman in *Absalom, Absalom!*, however, is probably Rosa. Her function as a figure of Sin is suggested, in part, by her resemblance to Clytie, another small, doll-like woman associated with keys, the color black, and with Cassandra. More telling, however, is Rosa's kinship with Sutpen. Like him she is cold, ruthless, vain, and proud; she too is linked with the serpent and with Satan's use of disguise; and she as well can wield a whip.[51]

Faulkner's depiction of the grim results of incest also follows the example of *Paradise Lost*. One consequence stressed by Milton is a loss of humanity—a descent into brutehood illustrated by the monstrous Hell Hounds engendered in Death's rape of his mother. In *Absalom, Absalom!* and *The Sound and the Fury*, the family lines terminate in a couple of animal-like idiots, poor brutes who are not actually the product of incest but who represent, in their affliction, the loss of authentic being that follows the Fall. Nor is the bestial metamorphosis the only expression of the bondage that the Fall entails. In *Absalom, Absalom!* the spiritual bondage that Sin creates is presented primarily in the metaphor of slavery, an institution that enthralls the enslaved and enslaver alike, but it is also evident, in both *Absalom, Absalom!* and *The Sound and the Fury*, in Faulkner's relegation of his nameless ones to a living Hell, whether it be the heat of Mississippi or the cold of Boston, the blighted garden of the Compsons or the rotting shell at Sutpen's Hundred.[52]

But the most terrible consequence of incest is death—the "grim and terrible" son that issues from the union of Satan and Sin. In *Absalom* it is Sutpen, "the evil's source and head," like Satan "the author of all ill," who embraces sin and sires death (*PL* II.381, X.832; *AA*, 18). One of these figures of death is his grandson, Charles Etienne, an identification that emerges in the justice's questioning of the boy in the courtroom; his words—" ' "What are you? Who and where did you come from?" ' "— are those of Satan confronting his son: "Whence and what are thou?" (*AA*, 203; *PL* II.681). Sutpen's Hundred, a product of Sutpen as much as any child, is also linked to Death; Rosa's description of its origins, her statement that Sutpen "*without warning upon the land*" "*Tore violently a plantation . . . tore violently,*" repeats Sin's recapitulation for Satan of the birth of Death: "Thine own begotten breaking violent way / Tore through my entrails" (*AA*, 9; *PL* II.782–83).

It is the portrait of Bon, however, that owes most to Milton's concept of Death. Sutpen's Hundred's introduction to Bon—"enclosed and surrounded by a sort of Scythian glitter"—echoes the evocation of Sutpen's ghost—"circumambient and enclosed by its effluvium of hell"—and stresses that Bon, like Death, is surely his father's son. This description also recalls Satan's return to Hell to celebrate his corruption of Adam and Eve, the scene in which the demon, "clad" in his "false glitter," gazes "round about him" at "the Stygian throng" (*AA*, 93, 13; *PL* X.448–55); in linking Bon with Satan's recent triumph on earth, a victory which means death to man, it gives added emphasis to the doom that Bon will call down upon the Sutpens.[53] In his retreat, in the face of Sutpen's opposition, to a passive spectator who "seems to hover shadowy, almost substanceless" over the family struggle, Bon resembles more than ever amorphous Death: "The other shape, / If shape it might be call'd that shape had none / . . . Or substance might be call'd that shadow seem'd" (*PL* II.666–69; *AA*, 93). Most of all, however, Bon is linked to Death by the dreadful grimace that punctuates his conversations with the snake-like lawyer before his departure for Mississippi and also appears repeatedly in the scenes at the Carolina encampment, shortly before his death; "the smiling that wasn't smiling but was just something you were not supposed to see beyond" recalls of course Death's gruesome grin: "and Death / Grinn'd horrible a ghastly smile, to hear / His famine should be fill'd" (*AA*, 308; *PL* II.845–47).

Sutpen's other son, Henry, also serves as a figure of Death, a function that is revealed primarily at the Confederate camp in Carolina, where Sutpen directs Henry down the road to fratricide. As the multitude of Milton borrowings suggests, this act closely parallels Satan's release of Sin and Death into the world. When Sutpen rises from his chair at Henry's entrance into the tent, "*his shadow swooping high and huge up the canvas wall,*" he is Satan, who "soars / Up to the fiery concave tow'ring high," as he nears his confrontation with Sin and Death at the gates of Hell (*AA*, 352; *PL* II.634–35). At first Sutpen is not recognized by his son, who looks only at the uniform and not at the face; in Book X, following the reunion with Sin and Death (who had not known his father at an earlier meeting), Satan ascends the throne of Hell in the guise of an "Angel militant" and "round about him saw unseen" (*PL* X.488). There is between Sutpen and Henry a "*rapport of blood*" that renders speech unnecessary and allows a wordless communication which seems to Henry both "*logical and natural*"; similarly, in Book X, Sin and Death feel themselves drawn to their sire, attracted by "some connatural force" that unites "things of like kind" (*AA*, 353; *PL* X.245–49). Like Sin and Death, Henry is identified also with Satan, for he, like them, will serve as an arm of the father's revenge. Making his way back to the bivouac fires after the meeting with Sutpen, Henry retraces his steps, repeats—haltingly, however—

the earlier journey when he *"walks alone through the darkness along a rutted road"* (*AA*, 352); as he prepares to return to Hell in Book X, Satan informs his progeny that he will this time "Descend through Darkness, on your Road with ease" (*PL* X.394). Finally, just before he confronts Bon, Henry is likened to Death as he pauses beside a pine tree and looks *"up at the shabby shaggy branches like something in wrought iron spreading motionless against the chill vivid stars of early spring"*; ordered by Satan to descend to earth upon the bridge that they have "wrought," Sin and Death "with speed / Thir course through thickest Constellations held / Spreading thir bane" (*AA*, 355; *PL* X.410–12). Henry embarks now on such a journey.

In *Absalom, Absalom!*, as elsewhere in Faulkner, the importance of the incest theme is dependent on and evident in the emphasis that is placed on the Fall—a lapse that is indicated, here as before, by images of descent and departure, of falling, of the frozen moment, and a suspension of time. Nowhere is this stress on the Fall more pronounced than in the story of Sutpen's life, and nowhere in the story is the imagery more pervasive than in the account of Sutpen's symbolical fall into life. Leaving an Edenic existence in the mountains of West Virginia, the Sutpen family "fell" into the world, "tumbled head over heels back to Tidewater by sheer altitude, elevation and gravity, as if whatever slight hold the family had had on the mountain had broken" (*AA*, 222–23). As he descends, Sutpen is confronted with the realities of life: sex, birth, death, slavery, greed, cruelty, the concept of caste and class. On the journey down, he not only becomes alienated from the natural world, but he suffers as well a loss of identity: "he knew neither where he had come from nor where he was nor why" (*AA*, 227). It is the same bewilderment which is experienced by the newly created Eve, who awakes in Eden and wonders "where / and what I was, whence thither brought, and how"; and the same confusion which Adam, awaking to life, expresses in similar words: "But who I was, or where, or from what cause, / Knew not . . ." (*PL* IV.451–52; *PL* VIII.270–71).

But the one image of the Fall that predominates in *Absalom, Absalom!* is that of the arrested moment, a suspension in time which precedes the fall into life, into sex, or into death. The Sutpen family's descent from the mountains, a fall into time, is described as "a sort of dreamy and destinationless locomotion . . . during which they did not seem to progress at all but just to hang suspended while the earth itself altered . . . rising about them like a tide . . ." (*AA*, 224–25).[54] Judith's adolescence, a preface to the fall into womanhood and sex, is a time when she exists in a state of "nebulous suspension"—dreamy, detached, impervious, and inaccessible (*AA*, 67).[55] Periods of suspension precede the fall into death:

the four years of "durance" before Henry shoots Bon, Ellen's two years in her "darkened room," the three years of Mr. Coldfield's exile in the attic, and the forty-three years of Rosa's "static outrage." In fact, as the imagery in Faulkner sometimes suggests, the whole of life may be regarded as one tremendous pause or hiatus; for we are at birth condemned to death, and life itself is but a suspended sentence, "one constant and perpetual instant" before the "arras-veil" (*AA*, 142). The most memorable image of suspension in *Absalom*, however, describes the calm that precedes the disaster of the Civil War:

> Because the time now approached . . . when the destiny of Sutpen's family which for twenty years now had been like a lake welling from quiet springs into a quiet valley and spreading, rising almost imperceptibly and in which the four members of it floated in sunny suspension, felt the first subterranean movement toward the outlet, the gorge which would be the land's catastrophe too . . . (*AA*, 73–74)

It is an image that evokes the "standing lake" of Milton's deluge: then all the "fountains of the Deep" will make the ocean overflow until "inundation rise" above the hills and the "Mount of Paradise" is moved from its place, pushed "Down the great River to the op'ning Gulf" (*PL* XI.825–33). The War, like the Flood, will be God's way of punishing man for yet another repetition of the original sin: the white Southerner's enslavement of his black brother.

The imagery of suspension also figures prominently in *The Unvanquished* and *Go Down, Moses*, and there too it signals a fall into disaster and death. In *Go Down, Moses*, Ike McCaslin pauses to reflect at "the crest of the knoll" where Sam and Lion lie buried, and there he experiences an epiphany of sorts—a Whitmanesque vision which denies the existence of death and postulates instead an immortality achieved through the body's absorption into the natural world. This vision, however, is followed immediately by images of the Fall: Ike's encounter with the snake, ancient symbol of sin and death; the sudden appearance of the Gum Tree, "alive" with whirling squirrels; and finally, the sight of Boon hammering madly at his gun, lost to all reason in the lust of greed.[56] In *The Unvanquished* a suspension of time usually precedes the fall into a very specific catastrophe, some kind of encounter between the Southerner and his foes: the confrontation of Colonel Sartoris, Ringo, and Bayard with the Yankee troops at the foot of the hill; the conflict at the river between migrating blacks and the Northern forces holding the bridge; Ringo's and Bayard's killing of the scalawag Grumby; and Bayard's unarmed vanquishment of the carpetbagger Redmond.

The sense of suspension in *Absalom, Absalom!*, however, is not conveyed solely by its imagery; it is evoked also by the book's structure and style. A feeling of stasis, of a failure to progress, is created by the circularity of the narratives, as they return time and again to certain central events; and by the author's practice of shuttling back and forth among the narrators, refusing to move in an orderly fashion from one monologue to the next. A similar sensation is evoked by the manner in which action is often attenuated, the completion of an act—the delivery of Wash's message to Rosa or the reading of Mr. Compson's letter—postponed for dozens or even hundreds of pages. A sense of arrested time is created, as well, by Faulkner's unusually full and complex style of writing, in which the sentences are long and involved, the subject often delayed and the meaning withheld, where syntactic forms are balanced one against the other, and conflicting words are forced together in uneasy unions. The most extreme example, perhaps, of the complexity of Faulkner's writing is found in Part IV of "The Bear"; here Isaac McCaslin, in a sentence extending over six entire pages and including a parenthesis that is two pages in length, relates his discovery of old Carother's incest with his daughter Tomasina—"the specific tragedy which had not been condoned and could never be amortized" (*GDM*, 266).

The key to Faulkner's use of arrested time is found once again in a reading of *Paradise Lost*. Here too there appears the hiatus that precedes a fall: the period on the summit of the hill when Michael instructs Adam in the future of mankind—a time that delays for a while Adam's expulsion from Eden and fall into the world; and also the period of Adam's "life prolong'd"—that time between the first transgression and the implementation of the sentence of death incurred by the Fall. This suspension of time is a gift of God, a period of grace which will allow Adam, not to prevent the fall which will follow, inevitably, but to ameliorate or even reverse its effects. As Michael tells Adam, the history he reveals is meant to fortify Adam for the life ahead and to prepare him for the death that awaits:

> Ere thou from hence depart, know I am sent
> To show thee what shall come in future days
> To thee and to thy Offspring; good with bad
> Expect to hear, supernal Grace contending
> With sinfulness of Men; thereby to learn
> True patience, and to temper joy with fear
> And pious sorrow, equally inur'd
> By moderation either state to bear,
> Prosperous or adverse: so shalt thou lead
> Safest thy life, and best prepar'd endure
> Thy mortal passage when it comes.
> (*PL* XI.356–66)

The period of Adam's temporary reprieve from death will provide him, additionally, with the opportunity to repent and to make amends, thereby achieving his redemption:

> *Adam,* Heav'n's high behest no Preface needs:
> Sufficient that thy Prayers are heard, and Death,
> Then due by sentence when thou didst transgress,
> Defeated of his seizure many days
> Giv'n thee of Grace, wherein thou mayst repent,
> And one bad act with many deeds well done
> May'st cover: well may then thy Lord appeas'd
> Redeem thee quite from Death's rapacious claim. . . .
> (*PL* XI.251–58)

Although the images of suspension appear in virtually every book that Faulkner wrote, they reveal their Miltonic roots most clearly in a sketch entitled "The Hill" and in its expanded version, "Nympholepsy." In both works a young itinerant worker pauses in quiet contemplation at the top of a hill. In "The Hill" this brief pause almost yields some sort of epiphany, but the moment of illumination escapes "the terrific groping of his mind," leaving him unaware of the fact even that "he had been eluded."[57] In "Nympholepsy," too, he fails to grasp the message of the moment, but the nature of the knowledge is made clearer—at least to us. We see in the young man's confused thoughts and sensations, as he pauses, a dim awareness of the effects of the Fall: the perception of a change in nature, once holy and sanctified and now hostile and threatening; the sense of an alteration also within himself, his "once-clean instincts" turned to "swinish" lust; an apprehension of the remoteness or indifference of God; a fear of the imminence of death, of an "abrupt and dreadful annihilation"; and a "sensation of imminent displeasure and anger, of a Being whom he had offended."[58] These impressions, however, have but a fleeting effect; the fear of death, even, fading from his thoughts as he descends the hill, Faulkner's young man profits little from the experience—unlike Adam and, perhaps Faulkner is saying, all too much like most of us.[59]

Faulkner's application of the Miltonic concept of suspension is found also in his treatment of art. As Faulkner sees it, art is associated with the hiatus in a variety of ways. It has the ability to preserve the past in the present; it is able to freeze time—"to arrest motion, which is life" and to "hold it fixed."[60] As Quentin reads the "faint and spidery script" of Bon's letter to Judith, the "dead tongue," silenced for fifty years, speaks once again (*AA,* 129). Art halts time in the sense that it creates a pause in the listener's life; the telling of the tale, as well as the story itself, constitutes a segment of frozen time. As Quentin listens to the ceaseless flow of words in Rosa's hot and airless little house, the sun seems hardly to have moved; the room at Harvard where Sutpen's story is reconstructed by Quentin and Shreve is a place remote and removed—a "snug monastic coign," "a dreamy and heatless alcove" (*AA*, 258). In its concern with the eternal verities, art triumphs over time, promoting that which is stable and changeless in the flux of life and, thus, helping man to endure. The old commissary ledgers of *Go Down, Moses,* which record "the injustice and a little at least of its amelioration and restitution," function much as the Bible to which they are juxtaposed (*GDM*, 261). And art, which is eternal, has the power to bestow upon its creator some measure of its own immortality. In entrusting Bon's letter to Mrs. Compson and thereby preserving some record of her story, Judith hopes "to make that scratch, that undying mark on the blank face of the oblivion to which we are all doomed" (*AA*, 129). Similarly, Cecelia Farmer in *Requiem for a Nun,* scratching her name and the date on the jailhouse window, makes her mark on the wall of oblivion—that "Crystal wall" that looks on the void. A defense against death is found in art and even, beyond that, the possibility of a triumph over the grave. Like the vision evoked by Michael on the top of the hill or the history that is related to Adam there, art in Faulkner has as its purpose the endurance and the redemption of man.[61]

In the achievement of this purpose, an important part is played by the incest theme, whose function it is to impress upon us the ugliness of evil and the need for change. In *Absalom, Absalom!* it discharges its duty admirably. In this novel, which includes several varieties of incest that touch on five members of the Sutpen-Coldfield family, incest is presented in a stronger and harsher light than before. It is linked with homosexuality, repudiation of kinship, slavery, and fratricide—associations which clearly do not lighten its own load of blame. It is depicted in more realistic terms in *Absalom,* where it becomes a real possibility in the lives of the characters, a treatment that gives to the theme a new urgency. More clearly than ever, it signals an end, the collapse of the Sutpen domain plainly paralleling the fall of the South. The flaw, the deep crack, that brings down the edifice at Sutpen's Hundred and the structure of Southern society as well, is the sin of an arrogant and self-serving pride that leads to a denial of brotherly love.

5

Conclusion

The theme of incest, then, pervades much of the work of William Faulkner. It emerges very early in his writing and appears in a number of his books: *Mosquitoes, As I Lay Dying, Sanctuary, Go Down, Moses, The Unvanquished, Pylon, Knight's Gambit, The Wild Palms.* It is a major theme in *Flags in the Dust, The Sound and the Fury,* and *Absalom, Absalom!,* all of which belong to the period of his greatest creativity. *Flags in the Dust* is the first book of the Yoknapatawpha cycle; *The Sound and the Fury* and *Absalom, Absalom!* are the two most important works in the canon. The theme touches virtually all of the great families of Yoknapatawpha; a list of those implicated in incest includes the Benbows, the Sartorises, Compsons, Sutpens, McCaslins, and Backuses. It contains as well the Bundrens, a family of yeoman-class farmers who own the bit of land they till. The theme of incest also appears in the relationships of people, rich and poor, who live outside the confines of Faulkner's apocrypha: *Mosquitoes'* Pat and Josh Robyn, Charlotte Rittenmeyer and her brother in *The Wild Palms,* Laverne and her brother-in-law in *Pylon.* These relationships illustrate a variety of incestuous combinations: brother-sister (which predominates), father-daughter, stepmother and stepson, stepfather and stepdaughter, sister and brother-in-law, and cousins.

As the pervasiveness of incest in the works indicates, the theme is an important one for Faulkner; as a metaphor for the original evil, it is a vehicle for the concept which is the focus of all his writing: the Fall of man. This metaphor is not without its difficulties, but these are alleviated by Faulkner's depiction of incest in realistic terms that support and clarify its symbolical import. In our efforts to discover in these realistic details Faulkner's attitude toward incest and its function in his works, we are aided, in turn, by knowledge garnered from nonliterary disciplines, such as anthropology, psychology, and history, that deal with the occurrence of incest in the actual world.

An acquaintance with the discoveries of anthropologists helps us in broadening the perspective we take to the study of incest, and it can also assist us in such specific ways as the interpretation of particular characters and passages. Quentin's ambivalence toward sex is better understood in the light of Brain's theory that the fear of incest or the fear of death can cause the fear of sex. Versh's passage on the bluegum is explained—and also something of Benjy's role in the novel—when it is viewed as a variation on Freud's Myth of the Primal Horde, a quasi-anthropological explanation for the origin of the incest taboo. Bon's inability to stomach miscegenation when he could swallow the incest is more terrible than ever when we recall that, according to anthropologists' theories, incest is inimical to civilization itself. The most important contribution anthropologists make to our understanding of incest in Faulkner, however, is to clarify our perception of this act as a preface to catastrophe, a view which very much agrees with Faulkner's concept of incest as a metaphor for the Fall. A survey of Faulkner's works reveals that incest is associated with a variety of disasters: dismal, sterile lives; catastrophic marriages; promiscuous behavior; alcoholism; exile; fratricide; and suicide.

Some familiarity with psychologists' profiles of incest offenders can sharpen the outlines of Faulkner's incestuous characters, who exhibit many of the same characteristics. Like the participants in actual cases of incest, Narcissa and Caddy act as surrogate mothers, a role which points to sibling incest's function as the oedipus-once-removed. In his affliction, Benjy demonstrates the inwardness, regression, and failure to grow that are found in incest cases; and he recalls the widespread belief that incest produces mentally defective offspring. Also, the absence of communion within the incestuous family and its alienation from the community are terribly evident in the lives of the Sutpens and the Compsons. And there appear in Faulkner's fiction many other characteristics observed in actual cases of incest: motherlessness, role violation, exploitation, homosexuality, repression, and identity crisis.

A historical perspective is helpful primarily to a reading of *Absalom, Absalom!* Southern history throws some light on Henry and Bon and their relationship; we see that Henry fits the description of the representative Southern heir and that Henry and Bon typify the two strains—puritanism and hedonism—that meet in the Southern psyche. Of greater significance is the likelihood that there is a correlation between Sutpen's story and that of Lothar II of Lotharingia—that Lothar may have served as a model for Henry's Duke John of Lorraine or Charles the Bald as a source for Sutpen. Certainly, the lessons derived from the stories of the Carolingian kings are those found in the Sutpen tale—that incest, or even the suggestion or threat of it, destroys families and wrecks kingdoms. Most important, however, is the possibility that Henry VIII served as a model for Sutpen, providing a pattern for his arrogance and pride, his desperate desire to establish his line, and his willingness to employ even incest to do it.

From studies in anthropology, psychology, and history, we can see that Faulkner handles the theme of incest realistically. We can also see that his conclusions agree with theirs. These studies show that the purpose of the taboo is survival—the propagation of the species, the cohesion of society, and the integration of the individual. In his fiction, where he focuses on the violation of the ban and the destruction and disaster that follow in its wake, Faulkner reveals that the converse is horrifyingly true.

In his treatment of incest, however, Faulkner is indebted principally to literature. He drew from a variety of sources, and echoes (bearing on incest) appear in several works: W. Somerset Maugham and Lord Byron in *Flags in the Dust*, Oscar Wilde in *Sanctuary*, and Sherwood Anderson in *The Sound and the Fury*. But these echoes are faint ones. The major influences on the incest theme come from Milton and Mann. Those in *Flags in the Dust* derive chiefly from Mann and turn up primarily in Faulkner's emphasis on the duality of man. Like Mann, Faulkner concerns himself with man's inability to bring into some sort of harmony the two halves—the sense and spirit—of his being, a schism of the psyche in which thought represses feeling, and the emotions exact their revenge. Like Mann's Aschenbach, Horace represents the spiritual half of man while Narcissa, like Tadzio, typifies man's other half—the pole of sensation as opposed to thought. Supporting characters in both of the books represent and reveal those instincts which the protagonists have repressed and which eventually destroy them. In both of the works the fall from wholeness leads to ruin, a devastation that is adumbrated in the garden imagery of a fallen world.

But in his development of the theme of incest, Faulkner owes most to *Paradise Lost* and its concept of incest as a metaphor for the original sin. In Faulkner, as in Milton, this act is willful and deliberate and constitutes a revolt against God; it springs from pride, ambition, anger, and lust, from a sense of injured merit, and a desire for revenge. And in Faulkner also we find evil and sin and death personified, and Adamic and Eve-like characters drawn. In the sibling relationships, a less offensive incest conforming to that of Adam and Eve, we encounter Adamic types like Benjy and Quentin, the Eve-like figures of Caddy and her daughter. In the uglier, more exploitive relationships of intergenerational incest, there emerge the satanic figures of Jason and Sutpen. Types of Sin appear also in Faulkner, for there too Satan generates sin, the snaky sorceress revealed in the persons of Clytie, Eulalia, and Rosa. In their function as narrators, Faulkner's characters operate again on an allegorical level; in

The Sound and the Fury, particularly, they embody the various faculties of Milton's faculty psychology: sense, fancy, and reason. Faulkner's depiction of incest's grim consequences also follows the example of *Paradise Lost.* Here too the incest signals a descent into brutehood, a degeneration illustrated in the termination of the Compson and Sutpen family lines in two animal-like idiots. Faulkner's characters, too, suffer the bondage of Milton's sinners, their spiritual imprisonment presented in the metaphor of slavery and evident also in the relegation of these nameless ones to a living Hell. But the most terrible consequence is man's mortality, the grim amorphous figure of Death taking shape in *Absalom* as Charles Etienne, Henry, and Bon. In his depiction of the Fall—for which incest is the vehicle—Faulkner again reveals the influence of Milton. The image of the hill, which appears in virtually every book that Faulkner wrote, signals the descent into life, sex, pain, toil, and death; just as Eden's "top of speculation" witnesses Adam's and Eve's expulsion from Paradise and fall into the world. Also pointing to the Fall is Faulkner's use of the frozen moment, an image or concept present in the action of the stories, in Faulkner's attitude toward art, and in the author's suspended style. And its purpose for Faulkner is the same as for Milton: to provide a pause in which man can fortify himself for life, prepare for death, and achieve his redemption.

In Faulkner's own segment of frozen time—his books—this purpose is served admirably by the incest theme. In its realistic depiction, one that accords with the findings of nonliterary studies, and in its use as a metaphor for the original sin, incest brings home the horror of evil and announces the need for change.

Notes

Chapter 1

1. George Murdock, who surveyed 250 primitive societies in 1949 and found the taboo in all of them, is generally credited with establishing the universality of the sanctions against incest. See Karin C. Meiselman, *Incest: A Psychological Study of Causes and Effects with Treatment Recommendations* (San Francisco: Jossey-Bass, 1978), p. 4; R. H. Potvin, "Incest Taboo," in *New Catholic Encyclopedia*, VII, p. 420.

2. Meiselman, p. 2.

3. Claude Levi-Strauss and George Murdock, according to Fox, are among "the most recent and most forceful" proponents of this theory. See Robin Fox, *The Red Lamp of Incest* (New York: E. P. Dutton, 1980), p. 11. See also James Brain, *The Last Taboo: Sex and the Fear of Death* (Garden City, N. Y.: Anchor-Doubleday, 1979), p. 41.

4. For discussions of the origin and function of the incest taboo, see Brain, p. 164; Robin Fox, *Kinship and Marriage: An Anthropological Perspective* (Baltimore: Penguin Books, 1967), pp. 57–75; Fox, *Red Lamp*, pp. 4, 9–14; Blair and Rita Justice, *The Broken Taboo: Sex in the Family* (New York: Human Sciences Press, 1979), pp. 26–28, 36–37, 41; Margaret Mead, *Sex and Temperament in Three Primitive Societies* (New York: William Morrow, 1935), pp. 82–85; Meiselman, pp. 5–26; Potvin, p. 420; Luciano P. R. Santiago, *The Children of Oedipus: Brother-Sister Incest in Psychiatry, Literature, History, and Mythology* (Roslyn Heights, N. Y.: Libra Publishers, 1973), pp. 4–6, 174.

5. Justice, pp. 27, 39; Irving Kaufman, Alice Peck, and Conseulo Tagiuri, "The Family Constellation and Overt Incestuous Relations between Father and Daughter," *American Journal of Orthopsychiatry* 24 (1954): 266; Meiselman, pp. 41–42.

6. Ann W. Burgess et al., *Sexual Assault of Children and Adolescents* (Toronto: D. C. Heath and Company, 1978), pp. 17, 132-33; William Masters and Virginia Johnson, "Incest: The Ultimate Sexual Taboo," *Redbook*, April 1976, pp. 54–58; Meiselman, pp. 24–25, 75, 263; Santiago, p. 155.

7. Justice, pp. 57–104; Meiselman, pp. 83–312.

8. Burgess et al., pp. 134, 136; Susan Forward and Craig Buck, *Betrayal of Innocence: Incest and its Devastation* (Los Angeles: J. P. Tarcher, 1978), pp. 4, 23, 114, 163; Justice, pp. 169, 187; Kaufman, Peck, and Tagiuri, pp. 275, 277; Meiselman, pp. 52, 178, 184, 191, 192, 229–30, 281.

9. Two notable exceptions are the works of Richard von Krafft-Ebing and those of Sigmund Freud.

10. William Faulkner, *Faulkner in the University: Class Conferences at the University of Virginia, 1957–1958*, ed. Frederick L. Gwynn and Joseph L. Blotner (Charlottesville: University Press of Virginia, 1959), p. 268.

11. According to Marjorie Dunlap, who lived in Oxford from 1955–1979 and who had her information from a friend, Mary Alice Roi (Mrs. Dan Roi), who worked in the Oxford welfare office, the incidence of incest in Oxford was extremely high, particularly in the lower socio-economic class of the white population. Personal interview with Marjorie Dunlap, March, 1981; telephone interview, December, 1982.

12. This theory, which is held by the anthropologist Slotkin, is challenged however by Goodenough, another anthropologist. See Santiago, p. 36.

13. C. Suetonius Tranquillus, *The Lives of the Twelve Caesars*, trans. Alexander Thomson, revised T. Forester (London: George Bell and Sons, 1890), pp. 268–69.

14. See Gen. ii.21–25; Gen. v.17, 26; Gen. xix.30–38; Gen. xx.12; Gen. xxxviii.

15. In Leviticus and Deuteronomy, the following incestuous unions are prohibited: "those of son and mother, of a man with the wife of his father (Lev. xviii.8; Deut. xxvii.20), and with the mother of his wife (Deut. xxvii.23), of a man with his granddaughter or his wife's daughter or granddaughter (Lev. xviii.10, 17), of a man with his sister or half-sister (Lev. xviii.9; Deut. xvii.22; see, however, Gen. xx.12), of a nephew with his aunt (Lev. xviii.12–14; cf. Exod. vi.20), of a man with his daughter-in-law or with his sister-in-law (Lev. xviii.15, 16; xx.21). Penalties for incest were death (Lev. xx.11–17), excommunication (Lev. xviii.29), and being cursed (Deut. xxvii.20, 22–23), e.g., by being childless (Lev. xx.21)." See J. J. Davis, "Incest (in the Bible)," *New Catholic Encyclopedia*, VII, p. 419. In both the Old and New Testaments, instances of incest are noted and condemned: Amnon's rape of Tamar, his sister; Absalom's incest with his father's concubines; the marriages of Herod Antipas to his niece and to his sister-in-law; and the incest condemned by Paul of a man with his step-mother. See II Sam. xiii.1–32; II Sam. xvi.21–22; Mark vi.17–18; I Cor. v.1–12.

16. In the *Acta Sanctorum* are inscribed the names of no fewer than 150 brother and sister saints, most of them founders of monasteries and convents. See Santiago, p. 62.

17. Donald W. Cory and R. E. L. Masters, *Violation of Taboo: Incest in the Great Literature of the Past and Present* (New York: The Julian Press, 1963), p. 5.

18. For the story of Lothar, see Eleanor S. Duckett, *Alfred the Great* (Chicago: The University of Chicago Press, 1956), p. 38; Peter R. McKeon, *Hincmar of Laon and Carolingian Politics* (Urbana: University of Illinois Press, 1978), pp. 39–50; J. C. L. Simonde de Sismondi, *The French under the Merovingians*, trans. William Bellingham (London, 1850; rpt. New York: AMS Press, 1976), pp. 343–48; H. Gwatkin et al., *Germany and the Western Empire*, in *The Cambridge Medieval History* (New York: The MacMillan Company, 1922), III, 38–44. For Henry's history, see Arthur G. Dickens, *The English Reformation* (New York: Schocken Books, 1964); J. J. Scarisbrick, *Henry VIII* (Berkeley: University of California Press, 1968), pp. 147–350.

19. For his discussion of incest in history, a topic which has received very little attention elsewhere, I am indebted especially to Santiago, pp. 25–97.

20. Cory and Masters, p. 9; Peter L. Thorslev, Jr., "Incest as Romantic Symbol," *Comparative Literature Studies* 2 (1965): 44–45, 47–50.

21. Thorslev, pp. 41–42.

22. A similar message is contained in the New Testament, where Jesus, the redeemer of all sins, is revealed as the descendant of Tamar, a woman who bore twins to her father-in-law, Judah. See Gen. xxxviii.

23. Cory and Masters, p. 12. The incest theme appeared in earlier dramas such as Shakespeare's *Hamlet* and Beaumont and Fletcher's *A King and No King*, but it was treated there as a peripheral concern.

24. Thorslev, p. 49.

25. Faulkner's use of incest as a metaphor for original sin is noted in a very early essay by John Arthos, a distinguished Milton scholar. See "Ritual and Humor in the Writing of William Faulkner," *Accent* 9 (1948): 26.

26. John Milton, *Paradise Lost, in Complete Poems and Major Prose,* ed. Merritt Y. Hughes (Indianapolis: The Odyssey Press, 1957), II.648–814. All further references to this work appear in the text as *PL.*

27. While the "wedded bliss" of Adam and Eve could, conceivably, be considered incest as well, it usually represents the innocence that Faulkner's siblings hope to recover, paradoxically, through incest. It was perhaps this motive that Faulkner had in mind when he said, according to Ben Wasson, "that incest was not the horrible, hideous crime it was thought to be." Ben Wasson, *Count No 'Count: Flashbacks to Faulkner* (Jackson: University Press of Mississippi, 1983), p. 52. Almost always, however, Faulkner's use of incest harkens back to the postlapsarian love-making which is characterized by lust, self-interest, and excess.

28. William Faulkner, *Lion in the Garden: Interviews with William Faulkner, 1926–1962,* ed. James B. Meriwether and Michael Millgate (1968; rpt. Lincoln: University of Nebraska Press, 1980), p. 119; *William Faulkner's Library: A Catalogue* (Charlottesville: University Press of Virginia, 1964), p. 70.

29. See William Faulkner, *Soldier's Pay* (1926; rpt. New York: Liveright, 1951), pp. 136, 200. All further references to this work appear in the text as *SP.* William Faulkner, "The Leg," in *Collected Stories of William Faulkner* (1950; rpt. New York: Vintage-Random, 1977), p. 823. William Faulkner, *Mosquitoes* (1927; rpt. New York: Liveright, 1951), p. 116. All further references to this work appear in the text as *M.*

30. William Faulkner, *Flags in the Dust,* ed. and introd. Douglas Day (New York: Random House, 1973), p. 154. All further references to this work appear in the text as *FD.*

31. Beth Burch, "A Miltonic Echo in Faulkner's *The Hamlet;*" *Notes on Contemporary Literature* 8, No. 4, n. d., pp. 3–4. In this note, Burch calls attention to similarities between the "bucolic" interlude of Ike and the cow and Milton's "Elegia Quinta."

32. Millgate asserts, quite rightly, that this omission results in a misunderstanding of many of Faulkner's images and "an insufficiently generous conception of the whole scale and direction of his endeavor." See *The Achievement of William Faulkner* (1963; rpt. Lincoln: University of Nebraska Press, 1978), p. 162. In his article, "Faulkner's Masters," Millgate also stresses Faulkner's debt to European writers and is again silent on Milton. See *Tulane Studies in English* 23 (1978): 143–155. Adams states that Faulkner, like Eliot, intended for the borrowings in his work to be recognized, that he wanted the words to recall the context in which they had appeared; in this way he hoped to pack "more meaning into his work, more emotional value, and a richer reverberation

of cultural tradition." See Richard P. Adams, "The Apprenticeship of William Faulkner," *Tulane Studies in English* 12 (1962): 118. Another critic interested in sources who overlooks the Milton influence is M. Gidley. See "Some Notes on Faulkner's Reading," *American Studies* 4 (1970): 91–102.

33. Brooks has drawn analogies between a number of Faulkner's characters and those of Milton: Mink Snopes of *The Mansion* and Satan of *PL*; the narrator in *The Marble Faun* and "the character whom we hear speaking" in Milton's "L'Allegro"; The Spirit of Autumn in *The Marionettes* and the Attendant Spirit of *Comus*; Harry Wilbourne of *The Wild Palms* and Milton's Adam in *Paradise Lost*. See Cleanth Brooks, *William Faulkner: Toward Yoknapatawpha and Beyond* (New Haven: Yale University Press, 1978), pp. 4, 37, 217; Cleanth Brooks, *William Faulkner: The Yoknapatawpha Country* (1963; rpt. New Haven: Yale University Press, 1977), p. 243. Brooks also sees in both Faulkner and Milton an impatience with organized religion. *Toward Yoknapatawpha and Beyond*, p. 243.

34. Vickery also points out the continued repetition in history of the original sin and the emergence of a pattern of redemption. *The Novels of William Faulkner: A Critical Interpretation* (1959; rev. ed. Baton Rouge: Louisiana State University Press, 1964), pp. 131–32.

35. In Milton's concept of evil and that of Faulkner in The Snopes trilogy, Adams finds a number of similarities: the idea that evil "on itself shall back recoil"; the depiction of the various Snopes, like that of Satan's followers, as separate and independent aspects of evil—Mink drawn as a Moloch-like character, Clarence as a Belial, and Montgomery Ward as a Mammon. See Percy G. Adams, "Humor as Structure and Theme in Faulkner's Trilogy," *Wisconsin Studies in Contemporary Literature* 5 (1964): 208–209. Aiken sees Jason as a character who is, like Satan, impelled by a " 'sense of injured merit,' " as a man who is envious, vengeful, egocentric, willful, and defiant. David Aiken, "The 'Sojer Face' Defiance of Jason Compson," *Thought* 52 (1977): 192–94. Albert J. Guerard finds in the styles of both Faulkner and Milton the following elements: "lyrical extravagance and running rythms," the extended simile and esoteric allusion," oxymorons, inverted syntax, long periodic sentences, the balancing of clauses, an absence of punctuation. See "The Faulknerian Voice," in *The Maker and the Myth: Faulkner and Yoknapatawpha, 1977,* ed. Evans Harrington and Ann J. Abadie (Jackson: University Press of Mississippi, 1978), pp. 40–42. Hopper in "Faulkner's Paradise Lost," which fails to deliver the comparison that its title seems to promise, has little to say about Faulkner's debt to Milton beyond the following brief observations: that Faulkner's failure to depict the restored Paradise reveals a despair that Milton did not know; that Faulkner's work, like Milton's, is the product of his "own inner conflict with the world about him"; that Faulkner's disgust at the ugliness of sin constitutes a "Miltonic dissent from the evils of the world"; and that Sutpen resembles Satan. Vincent F. Hopper, "Faulkner's Paradise Lost," *Virginia Quarterly Review* 23 (1947): 405, 408, 412.

36. Brooks, *Yoknapatawpha Country,* pp. 131–32; Millgate, p. 96; Vickery, p. 38; John W. Hunt, *William Faulkner: Art in Theological Tension* (Syracuse, N. Y.: Syracuse University Press, 1965), p. 117; Andre Bleikasten, *The Most Splendid Failure: Faulkner's "The Sound and the Fury"* (Bloomington: Indiana University Press, 1976), p. 115; Hyatt H. Waggoner, *William Faulkner: From Jefferson to the World* (Lexington: University of Kentucky Press, 1959), p. 48.

37. Vickery, p. 98; William Van O'Conner, *The Tangled Fire of William Faulkner* (New York: Gordian Press, 1968), p. 98.

38. Lee Jenkins, *Faulkner and Black-White Relations: A Psychoanalytic Approach* (New York: Columbia University Press, 1981), pp. 56–57, 204–205.

39. As Minter sees it, Faulkner's art, like Elmer's, emerges from his secret longings for the "dark mother." Minter finds further evidence of the incestuous impulse in Faulkner in Joan Williams' *The Wintering*, a fictionalized version of her relationship with Faulkner; here an aging author says to the aspiring young writer he loves, " 'I know I was the father you wanted. We've committed incest then. That alone will hold us together.' " See *William Faulkner: His Life and Work* (Baltimore: The Johns Hopkins University Press, 1980), pp. 101, 103, 230–31.

40. John T. Irwin, *Doubling & Incest / Repetition & Revenge: A Speculative Reading of Faulkner* (Baltimore: The Johns Hopkins University Press, 1975), pp. 1, 157, 158, 160.

41. Earle Labor, "Faulkner's *The Sound and the Fury*," *Explicator* 17 (1959): item 30; Marvin Morillo, "Faulkner's *The Sound and the Fury*," *Explicator* 24 (1966): item 50; Robert J. Kloss, "Faulkner's *As I Lay Dying*," *American Imago* 38 (1981): 429–444.

42. Albert J. Guerard, *The Triumph of the Novel: Dickens, Dostoevsky, Faulkner* (New York: Oxford University Press, 1976), p. 117; Arthos, p. 26; Kerry McSweeney, "The Subjective Intensities of Faulkner's *Flags in the Dust*," *The Canadian Review of American Studies* 8 (1977): 159; H. L. Weatherby, "Sutpen's Garden," *Georgia Review* 21 (1967): 363; George S. Lensing, "The Metaphor of Family in *Absalom, Absalom!*," *Southern Review* 11 (1975): 110; Beth V. Haury, "The Influence of Robinson Jeffers' 'Tamar' on *Absalom, Absalom!*," *Mississippi Quarterly* 25 (1972): 356–58.

43. Carvel Collins, "Miss Quentin's Paternity Again," *Texas Studies in Language and Literature* 2 (1960): 253–60; Louise Dauner, "Quentin and the Walking Shadow: The Dilemma of Nature and Culture," *Arizona Quarterly* 21 (1965): 167.

44. Mark Spilka, "Quentin Compson's Universal Grief," *Contemporary Literature* 2 (1970), p. 461; Lewis P. Simpson, "Sex and History: Origins of Faulkner's Apocrypha," in *The Maker and the Myth: Faulkner and Yoknapatawpha*, ed. Evans Harrington and Ann J. Abadie (Jackson: University Press of Mississippi, 1978), pp. 63–64; Labor, item 30.

45. Labor, item 30; Robert D. Jacobs, "Faulkner's Tragedy of Isolation," in *Southern Renascence: The Literature of the Modern South*, ed. Louis D. Rubin and Robert D. Jacobs (Baltimore: The Johns Hopkins Press, 1953), pp. 173–74; George Marion O'Donnell, "Faulkner's Mythology," *The Kenyon Review* 1 (1939): 285–99; rpt. in *Faulkner: A Collection of Critical Essays*, ed. Robert Penn Warren (Englewood Cliffs, N. J.: Prentice-Hall, 1966), p. 26; Peter Swiggart, "Moral and Temporal Order in *The Sound and the Fury*," *Sewanee Review* 61 (1953): 224; Charles D. Peavy, " 'Did You Ever Have a Sister?'—Holden, Quentin and Sexual Innocence," *Florida Quarterly* 1 (1968): 84; Spilka, p. 461.

Chapter 2

1. William Faulkner, *Selected Letters of William Faulkner*, ed. Joseph Blotner (1977; rpt. New York: Vintage-Random, 1978), p. 38.

2. Joseph Blotner, "William Faulkner's Essay on the Composition of *Sartoris*," *The Yale University Library Gazette* 47 (1973): 123.

3. Faulkner, *Faulkner in the University*, p. 285.

4. As Lewis Simpson notes, these concepts are present in some of Faulkner's earliest writing. In his explication of poems XLII and XXVI in *A Green Bough*, Simpson points out two important consequences of the Fall: "the modern rupture of sense and spirit"; and the "repression of the instinctive desires of the blood" which "paradoxically does not suppress man's cosmic 'crumb of fire' but, opposing, feeds it." See Simpson, "Sex and History," pp. 45–47.

5. Thus far, the possibility of a debt to *Death in Venice* in *Flags in the Dust* has not been explored. A link between Mann's works and Faulkner's has been suggested, briefly and generally, by Richard P. Adams and Donald M. Kartiganer; Joel Hunt, in a somewhat limited article, has pointed out parallels between Mann's "Mario and the Magician" and Faulkner's "An Error in Chemistry." These critics, however, make no mention of *Flags in the Dust* or *Death in Venice*. Although Richard Ziegfeld's dissertation focuses on Faulkner and Mann, it "makes no attempt to argue that they influenced one another." See Richard P. Adams, "The Apprenticeship," p. 141; Donald M. Kartiganer, *The Fragile Thread: The Meaning of Form in Faulkner's Novels* (Amherst: The University of Massachussetts Press, 1979), p. 183; Joel Hunt, "Thomas Mann and Faulkner: Portrait of a Magician," *Wisconsin Studies in Contemporary Literature* 8 (1967): 431–36; Richard Evan Ziegfeld, "A Methodology for the Study of Philosophy in Literature: Philosophy and Symbol in the Selected Works of William Faulkner and Thomas Mann," Diss. University of Texas, 1976, pp. v, 25.

6. Thomas Mann, *Death in Venice*, trans. Kenneth Burke (New York: Alfred A. Knopf, 1925), p. 17. The novella was published originally in Neue Rundschau in 1912. All further references in this work appear in the text as *DV*.

7. The influence of *Death in Venice* is quite apparent in *Elmer*. At summer's close, Elmer visits Venice, a city which looks like "voluptuous lace" and recalls "old fairy tales." There he encounters "boys with old cunning faces, in gaudy striped shirts" and pornography-vendors who barber on the side. A sense of the impurity of the place is conveyed by the greenness of the water and by a definite odor about the city, a smell associated with a prostitute's "stale, exciting flesh." While riding in a coffin-like gondola, Elmer experiences a hallucinatory dream which includes a number of features familiar to *DV*: three gray priests; a dead beggar with a "lean and age-chilled body"; hot-bellied rats, "keen and plump as death," that sniff at his "intimate parts"; torch bearers "antic as goats"; a "young naked boy whose skin has been daubed with vermilion." In jail, Elmer meets a young Italian named Angelo Marino who, like the prostitute, has a "brief snubbed nose." The two, who do not speak the same language, communicate with glances and smiles, and their relationship (patron and subordinate) contains hints of a homosexual interest. See William Faulkner, *Elmer, Mississippi Quarterly*, ed. James B. Meriwether, 36 (1983), 413–32.

8. Blotner, *William Faulkner's Library*, p. 107. H. T. Lowe-Porter's translation of *Death in Venice* appeared too late, however, to have served as a source for *Flags in the Dust*.

9. Faulkner, *Lion in the Garden*, pp. 49, 114, 250; Joseph Blotner, *Faulkner: A Biography*, 2 vols. (New York: Random House, 1974), pp. 787, 1119–20, 1693.

10. These lines actually appear in *Sartoris*. In the passage in *Flags in the Dust*, the con-

nection with *Death in Venice* is not as clearly indicated: " 'Venice is a lovely place,' he added. 'Must take you there, some day' " (*FD*, 147). For the most part, however, the Mann influence is more pronounced in *Flags in the Dust*, the original version of the novel, than it is in *Sartoris*, the much-abridged version which Ben Wasson edited without Faulkner's assistance. The excised material includes the story of Horace's affair with Joan Heppleton and that of Snopes's visit to Minnie Sue, and it elaborates on the relationship between Horace and Narcissa. See William Faulkner, *Sartoris* (1929; rpt. New York: Signet, 1964), p. 141.

11. Thomas Mann, "The Blood of the Walsungs," in *Death in Venice and Seven Other Stories*, trans. H. T. Lowe-Porter (1930: rpt. New York: Vintage-Random, 1963), p. 297. "The Blood of the Walsungs" was originally published in 1905. Mann's continued interest in incestuous twins is evident in the appearance of Wilingis and Sibylla in *Holy Sinner*, his version of the Pope Gregory story, published 1951.

12. William Faulkner, *Sanctuary: The Original Text*, ed. Noel Polk (New York: Random House, 1981), p. 16. All further references to this work appear in the text as *SOT*.

13. William Faulkner, *Light in August* (1932; rpt. New York: Random House, 1967), pp. 177–78. All further references to this work appear in the text as *LA*.

14. Morillo, item 50.

15. William Faulkner, "There Was a Queen," in *Collected Stories*, p. 740.

16. The Tudor architecture of the house reminds us of the lusty and incestuous Henry VIII, of the House of Tudor, and the Victorian modifications recall the sexual repressiveness of the nineteenth century.

17. Luciano P. R. Santiago states that the incest of siblings often represents "the sexual fulfillment of the Oedipus-once-removed." John T. Irwin also points out that the sister, in cases of sibling incest, frequently serves as a substitute for the mother. Santiago, p. 7; Irwin, p. 43.

18. Faulkner was, in fact, an admirer of Wilde's art. Blotner notes his "taste for the work of Oscar Wilde"; and he states that Faulkner signed his copy of Wilde's *Salome: A Tragedy in One Act*, a sure sign of his appreciation of the volume. See Blotner, *A Biography*, I, pp. 265, 296.

19. In his recent book, John T. Matthews misreads the description of the Benbow garden and misinterprets the role of Horace's and Narcissa's father. Will Benbow does not, as Matthews maintains, destroy "an unruly flower bed" and thus "uphold the order of culture"; he does not "obliterate the narcissistic, incestuous desire that would naturally flourish between his children." See *The Play of Faulkner's Language* (Ithaca: Cornell University Press, 1982), pp. 51–52.

20. William Faulkner, *Sanctuary* (1931; rpt. New York: Vintage-Random House, 1967), pp. 15–16. All further references to this work appear in the text as *S*.

21. Another echo of this passage, which compares the forbidden fruit to milk and to fennel, is heard I believe in *The Sound and the Fury*, where fennel is found in Benjy's garden.

22. Simpson, "Sex and History," pp. 45–47. Simpson states that "Both the Faun imprisoned in his 'marble bonds' and dreaming of pastoral freedom and the Pan who appears in his dreaming are chaste creatures" (47).

23. While he makes no claim that Mann influenced Faulkner, Lewis P. Simpson does note, in "Faulkner and the Legend of the Artist," the interest the two writers shared in the creative process, particularly in "the mystery of the identity of the writer." Simpson in fact takes as the epigraph of his article a line from *Death in Venice*: "Who shall unriddle the puzzle of the artist's nature?" See *Faulkner: Fifty Years after "The Marble Faun,"* ed. George H. Wolfe (Tuscaloosa: University of Alabama Press, 1976), pp. 69–75.

24. That incest always ends in destruction is a popular belief of long standing. Incest has been thought to cause "madness and death," natural disasters, "murders, suicides, and neurotic and psychotic breakdowns." See Thorslev, p. 45; Fox, *Red Lamp*, p. 6; Cory and Masters, p. 9. We are reminded also that the incestuous mating of Satan and Sin in *Paradise Lost* results in the birth of Death (II, 746-87).

25. This fusion of woman and water in an image of death appears repeatedly in Faulkner. Gail Morrison cites a number of works in which a woman mirrored in water or waiting in water signifies death: *Mayday, A Green Bough,* "Nympholepsy," *The Sound and the Fury.* See "Time, Tide, and Twilight: *Mayday* and Faulkner's Quest toward *The Sound and the Fury,*" *Mississippi Quarterly* 31 (1978); 351.

26. In an early essay, Faulkner makes clear the distinction between motionless water and rain: "One can imagine Hergesheimer submerging himself in Linda Condon as in a still harbor where the age cannot hurt him and where rumor of the world reaches him only as a far faint sound of rain." See "Books and Things: Joseph Hergesheimer" in *William Faulkner: Early Prose and Poetry,* ed. Carvel Collins (Boston: Little, Brown, 1962), p. 102.

27. W. Somerset Maugham, "Rain," in *East and West,* Vol. I of *The Complete Short Stories of W. Somerset Maugham* (Garden City, New York: Doubleday, 1934), p. 20. "Rain" was written in 1919. A Maugham influence is also suggested by the use of mosquitoes in both "Rain" and *Mosquitoes* to symbolize the "gadfly urge after the petty ignoble impulses" (*FD,* 288). Interestingly, Faulkner said in an interview that he found "a kinship between Maugham and Thomas Mann," and he mentioned specifically *Death in Venice* and what appeared to be "Rain" (the editors were uncertain as to the word Faulkner spoke, but they believed it to be "rain"). See *Lion in the Garden,* pp. 114–15. The rain in this scene in *Flags in the Dust* may also owe something to a folk belief mentioned in *The Golden Bough.* In his book Frazer states that the Toradjas of Celebes believed that rain could be produced by the copulation of sibling animals. I follow the authority of Santiago, p. 7.

28. Two other items from Mann's set of recurring features—the red tie and the straw hat— are quite conspicuous in *The Sound and the Fury.*

29. The function of twinning and incest as metaphors for disunion may well be derived from a legend Plato has Aristophanes relate in *The Symposium.* It describes an original hermaphroditic man split by Apollo into two monosexual parts, each half doomed to a lifetime of fruitless searching for the other. Vestiges of this myth are apparent, particularly, in Bayard's efforts, the first night of his visit with the MacCallums, to discover the source of his continued suffering: "That would account for it, would explain so much: that he too was dead and this was hell, through which he moved forever and ever with an illusion of quickness, seeking his brother who in turn was somewhere seeking him, never the two to meet" (*FD,* 315). The importance of twinning to Faulkner is evident in the frequency of its occurrence in the canon; twins appear among the Sartorises, McCaslins, Stevenses, Snopeses, Robyns, and MacCallums.

30. In Mann's "The Blood of the Walsungs," they merge also in the incest of the twins, Siegmund and Sieglinde. Additionally, in Pausanius (9.31.6), Irwin discovers a version of the Narcissus myth in which the youth is depicted as a twin, grief-stricken at the death of his beloved sister. See Irwin, p. 41.

31. In *Sanctuary* Clarence Snopes is likened to a "weak, acquisitive creature like a squirrel or a rat" (*S*, 169). See also Sanctuary, pp. 80, 90, 97; *The Wild Palms*, p. 40; *The Sound and the Fury*, pp. 158, 168, 172, 174.

32. Milton's *Paradise Lost* IV.800–809. Fiedler draws attention to the appearance of a similar gesture in Melville's *Pierre*. In a love scene featuring the protagonist and his half-sister Isabel, Pierre's " 'mouth wet her ear.' " According to Fiedler, the "presence of the serpentine horror of incest" is "implicit in the pressure of a damp mouth at the ear." Leslie A. Fiedler, *Love and Death in the American Novel* (1960; rev. ed. New York: Stein and Day, 1966), p. 421.

33. Some critics regard Bayard's attraction to Narcissa as a positive thing—an indication of his "will to live" and "to terminate his involvement in the Sartoris legend." See Melvin Backman, *Faulkner: The Major Years* (Bloomington: Indiana University Press, 1966), p. 8; Vickery, p. 22. It appears to me, however, that Bayard's attraction to Narcissa and her repose is one with his desire for death. In the calm following his hellish night at the MacCallums, Bayard certainly seems to equate peace, which "comes to all," with death (*FD*, 317).

34. McSweeney finds the relationship between "the principal subjective intensities"—"the power of sexuality and the power of the past"—to be "discontinuous and imperfectly focused" (159). It seems to me, however, that these two themes converge in the concept of original sin.

35. Philip Castille is mistaken in his belief that Narcissa, at the end of the novel, "reaches a maturity which involves a rejection of Sartoris escapsim." See " 'There Was a Queen' and Faulkner's Narcissa Sartoris," *Mississippi Quarterly* 28 (1975): 308.

36. The most recent news we have of Benbow does not appear to confirm this prognosis. In *The Mansion*, Charles Mallison refers to the seventeen-year-old heir of the Sartoris clan as "one of the best bird shots in the county"; in *Knight's Gambit*, we learn that Benbow serves during World War II as a commissioned officer in England. See William Faulkner, *The Mansion* (New York: Random House, 1959), p. 206; *Knight's Gambit* (New York: Random House, 1949), p. 240. The importance of these updates to a reading of *Flags in the Dust* is diminished, however, when we take into account not only their casual and cursory nature but also the distance that separates their publication dates from those of the earlier works. Bradford believes that Benbow will resist his mother's efforts to envelop him in her "solipsistic world," but unless we bow to the notes on Benbow in the later works, this seems uncertain at best. See Melvin E. Bradford, "Certain Ladies of Quality: Faulkner's View of Women and the Evidence of 'There Was a Queen,' " *The Arlington Quarterly* 1 (1967–68): 136.

Chapter 3

1. Faulkner, *Lion in the Garden*, p. 245.

2. William Faulkner, "An Introduction for *The Sound and the Fury*," ed. James B. Meriwether, *Southern Review* 8 (1972): 710.

3. Faulkner, *Lion in the Garden*, p. 147; *Faulkner in the University*, pp. 1, 32.

4. Faulkner, *Lion in the Garden*, p. 222.

5. Faulkner, *Faulkner in the University*, p. 275.

6. Carvel Collins, "The Interior Monologues of *The Sound and the Fury*," in *English Institute Essays 1952*, ed. Alan Downer (New York: Columbia University Press, 1954), pp. 29–56; revised and rpt. in *Studies in The Sound and the Fury*," comp. James B. Meriwether (Columbus, Ohio: Charles E. Merrill, 1970), p. 63; Carvel Collins, "The Pairing of *The Sound and the Fury* and *As I Lay Dying*," *Princeton University Library Chronicle* 18 (1957): 116–18; Lawrence E. Bowling, "Faulkner and the Theme of Innocence," *Kenyon Review* 20 (1958): 468, 475; Walter Brylowski, *Faulkner's Olympian Laugh: Myth in the Novels* (Detroit: Wayne State University Press, 1968), p. 69; Vickery, pp. 30–31; Maurice Coindreau, Traduction et preface, *Le Bruit et la fureur* (1938; rpt. Paris: Gallimard, 1949), pp. 9-12; Millgate, *The Achievement*, p. 91.

7. Brooks, *Yoknapatawpha Country*, pp. 326–31.

8. William Faulkner, *The Hamlet* (1940; rpt. New York: Random House, 1964), pp. 181, 186. All further references to this work appear in the text as *H*. In an article on Faulkner's sources, Richard Adams cites these passages as evidence of the influence of the troubador poets on Faulkner. They appear to me, however, to owe much to Milton. See "Faulkner: The European Roots," in *Faulkner: Fifty Years after "The Marble Faun*," ed. George H. Wolfe (Tuscaloosa: University of Alabama Press, 1976), pp. 34–35.

9. Carvel Collins maintains that "the three Compson sons, Benjy, Quentin, and Jason, amalgamate at a symbolic level into one son," but he believes that this Compson son represents Christ, that the experiences of Benjy, Quentin, and Jason are "symbolically parallel" to those of Christ in His Passion Week. See "The Pairing," pp. 116–17.

10. William Faulkner, "An Introduction to *The Sound and the Fury*," in *A Faulkner Miscellany*, ed. James B. Meriwether (Jackson: University Press of Mississippi, 1974), p. 160.

11. In the segment describing Ike's love for the cow, the association of the two books and the two characters is suggested, certainly, in the comparison of the "sound and fury" of the storm to "the abrupt and unplumable tantrum of a child," a passage which recalls particularly the conclusion of *The Sound and the Fury* (*H*, 185). Additionally, Benjy and Ike resemble one another in physical ways, such as their awkward, bear-like gait.

12. In this episode of Ike and the cow, Beth Burch also finds a Miltonic echo, but it is "Elegia Quinta," not *Paradise Lost*, which she cites as the influence on Faulkner. See "A Miltonic Echo in Faulkner's *The Hamlet*," *Notes on Contemporary Literature*, 8, No. 4, pp. 3–4.

13. William Faulkner, *The Sound and the Fury* (1929; rpt. New York: Random House, 1966), p. 3. All further references to this work appear in the text as *SF*.

14. Bleikasten, *The Most Splendid Failure*, p. 79. Faulkner himself makes it clear that the attack was sexual in nature in a letter to Ben Wasson, where he writes that Benjy "tries to rape a young girl and is castrated." See *Selected Letters*, p. 44.

15. Irving Howe, who first pointed out the significance of these passages, maintains that

the golf ball is "the dominant symbol in the Benjy section." See *William Faulkner: A Critical Study* (Chicago: University of Chicago Press, 1951), p. 172. The importance which Faulkner himself attached to the image of the golf ball is evident in the typescript of *SF* which was revised to include eleven new passages on Luster's efforts to find a golf ball. See Blotner, *Faulkner,* I, p. 589.

16. Sigmund Freud, *Totem and Taboo: Resemblances between the Psychic Lives of Savages and Neurotics,* trans. and introd. A. A. Brill (New York: Moffat, Yard, 1918), pp. 234–36. Although Faulkner himself stated that he was not "familiar with" Freud, he was probably acquainted with his ideas. Carvel Collins maintains that Faulkner heard Freudian theories discussed at length not only in the New Orleans literary group with which he and Anderson associated but also in conversations at Oxford with Phil Stone. Collins claims, furthermore, that he had this information directly from members of the New Orleans group and from Stone. See Faulkner, *Faulkner in the University,* p. 268; Collins, "Interior Monologues," p. 63.

17. This point is made in an old Negro folk rhyme:

> Blue gums an' black eyes:
> Run 'roun an' tell lies.
> Liddle head, liddle wit;
> Big long head, not a bit.

See Newbell Niles Puckett, *Folk Beliefs of the Southern Negro* (Chapel Hill: North Carolina University Press, 1926), p. 74.

18. William Faulkner, *As I Lay Dying* (1930; rpt. New York: Random House, 1964), pp. 63–64. All further references to this work appear in the text as *AILD*.

19. See Justice, pp. 80, 120, 187; Meiselman, pp. 93, 127–28, 264, 268; Burgess et al., p. 134; Forward and Buck, p. 4; Kaufman, Peck and Tagiuri, pp. 270, 275.

20. Rollo May, *Man's Search for Himself* (1953; rpt. New York: Dell, 1980), p. 134; Erich Fromm, *The Sane Society* (New York: Rinehart, 1955), p. 46; Justice, p. 28.

21. May, p. 134; Justice, p. 28.

22. Justice, p. 26; Meiselman, p. 15; Fox, *Kinship and Marriage,* p. 59.

23. Andrew Lytle, "The Working Novelist and the Mythmaking Process," *Daedalus* 98 (1959): 326–38; rpt. in *Myth and Literature: Contemporary Theory and Practice,* ed. John B. Vickery (Lincoln: Bison-University of Nebraska Press, 1966), pp. 102–103.

24. William Faulkner, Appendix, *The Sound and the Fury* (1946; rpt. New York: Modern Library-Random House, 1967), p. 411. All further references to this work appear in the text as *SFA*.

25. Jacobs, p. 171.

26. I follow the authority of Robert Jacobs, p. 174. Speaking from a different vantage-point, Rollo May and Robin Fox reach some of the same conclusions. See May, p. 136; Fox, *Kinship and Marriage,* p. 54.

27. Quentin's attraction to incest is attributed sometimes to rather commendable motives: the "desire to test the possibility of holiness"; the wish to "establish, if only negatively,

some meaning in the nature of things"; the effort "to transform meaningless degeneracy into significant doom." See Waggoner, p. 48; Hunt, p. 59; O'Donnell, p. 26.

28. A number of critics comment on the incestuous nature of Jewel's love for his mother, but the best discussion of this subject is found in Kloss. See Kloss, pp. 431–35.

29. This sonnet—which lashes out at the "bloody Piemontese that roll'd / Mother with Infant down the Rocks"—sounds the note of revenge in its opening line: "Avenge, O Lord, thy slaughter'd Saints."

30. A number of authorities discuss the part that isolation plays in incest—its role as a motive for initiating the relationship, as a condition which protects the incestuous family, and as a state which results from its practice. See Burgess et al., p. 22; Forward and Buck, p. 4; Thorslev, p. 50; Justice, pp. 63, 134–35, 169; Meiselman, pp. 108–109.

31. Several critics see in Quentin's attraction to incest the desire to return to childhood and the effort to escape the adult world. See Peavy, " 'Did You Ever Have a Sister?' " p. 84; O'Connor, p. 40; Bleikasten, *The Most Splendid Failure*, p. 115; Millgate, *The Achievment*, p. 96.

32. Perhaps Faulkner is recalling also the passage in Milton's *Comus* where the Elder Brother explains to the Second Brother the enthrallment of sin: "But he that hides a dark soul and foul thoughts / Benighted walks under the midday Sun; / Himself is his own dungeon" (382–84).

33. A number of critics believe that Darl harbors incestuous feelings for Dewey Dell. See Bleikasten, *Faulkner's "As I Lay Dying,"* p. 88; Irwin, p. 53; Kloss, pp. 439–40; Minter, p. 119.

34. See Leon F. Seltzer, "Narrative Function vs. Psychopathology: The Problem of Darl in *As I Lay Dying*," *Literature and Psychology* 25 (1975): 57; Kloss, p. 440; Charles Palliser, "Fate and Madness: The Determinist Vision of Darl Bundren," *American Literature* 49 (1978): 631.

35. Echoes of Milton's passage appear also in Faulkner's "Barn Burning," in the scene where Abner Snopes trails horse "droppings" across de Spain's imported rug: "Then with the same deliberation he turned; the boy watched him pivot on the good leg and saw the stiff foot drag round the arc of the turning, leaving a final long and fading smear." See *Collected Stories*, p. 12. In this scene, however, the creativity of God is parodied by the demonic Ab's destruction, as in *Paradise Lost* it often is by the evil of Satan.

36. William Faulkner, *The Wild Palms* (1939; rpt. New York: Modern Library-Random House, 1984), pp. 221, 204, 240. All further references to this work appear in the text as *WP*.

37. Irwin maintains, erroneously I believe, that it is a castration complex that unmans Quentin. According to Irwin, when Quentin puts the knife to the throat of his sister, an image of himself, he is threatened with castration, and Caddy becomes a castrator. See Irwin, pp. 46, 47.

38. It is possible that this fear of incest is responsible for Quentin's ambivalent attitude toward sex. According to anthropologist James Brain, "The phenomenon of wanting sex and yet being repelled by it because of an ingrained fear of incest is widespread" (110).

39. Speaking of Emily Grierson's desire for love and a family in "A Rose for Emily," Faulkner says, "and it was a natural instinct of—repressed which—you can't repress it—you can mash it down but it comes up somewhere else and very likely in a tragic form." See *Faulkner in the University,* p. 185.

40. David Herbert Lawrence, "Edgar Allen Poe," in *Studies in Classic American Literature* (William Heinemann, Ltd., 1923; rpt. in *The Recognition of Edgar Allen Poe: Selected Criticism since 1829,* ed. Erle W. Carlson, Ann Arbor: University of Michigan Press, 1966), p. 112.

41. Allen Tate, "Our Cousin, Mr. Poe," Poe Society of Baltimore, 7 October 1949; rpt. in *Poe: A Collection of Critical Essays,* ed. Robert Regan (Englewood Cliffs, N.J.: Prentice-Hall, 1967), p. 43.

42. According to James Brain, this association of sex with death occurs commonly in the human psyche and is responsible, in part at least, for the fear of sex (79–110).

43. Brooks, *Yoknapatawpha Country,* p. 332; *Toward Yoknapatawpha,* p. 215n.

44. In Poe also, as Leslie Fiedler points out, the impulse toward incest is one with the death-wish: "and the desire to embrace the sister-bride means for him first of all a yearning to *fall*—a perverse longing to plunge into the destructive embrace of his own image in a dark tarn" (415). Minter, however, does not equate the desire for incest, in Faulkner, with the wish for death; "Little Sister Death," as he sees it, signifies "an incestuous love forbidden on threat of death" (100).

45. Bleikasten notes the similarities between Jason and Quentin and points out a number of ways in which Jason's relationship with his niece parallels that of Quentin with his sister. See *The Most Splendid Failure,* pp. 158–60. Faulkner's purpose in drawing these parallels, Bleikasten seems to feel, is to present Quentin in a "truer color," that is, to reveal more fully the destructive effect he has on his sister. I am not convinced, however, that Quentin can be made accountable for the corruption of Caddy.

46. Bleikasten, *The Most Splendid Failure,* p. 160.

47. Sherwood Anderson, *Winesburg, Ohio* (1919; rpt. New York: Penguin Books, 1976), pp. 28, 33.

48. The headache's association with incestuous desire is reinforced by the similarity between Jason's comment on his headaches and Quentin's thoughts about castration: the wish never to have had "them."

49. David Aiken maintains that Jason resembles Milton's Satan in several respects: envy, vengefulness, "sense of injured merit," and defiance of God. See "The 'Sojer Face' Defiance of Jason Compson," *Thought* 52 (1977): 193–94. Faulkner himself says of Jason that he "represented complete evil. He's the most vicious character, in my opinion, I ever thought of." *Lion in the Garden,* p. 146.

50. Obsessed by what he believes Quentin has cost him and therefore owes him, Jason regards his niece with a greedy and a possessive eye. Such an attitude is not uncommon in the incestuous father, who sees his daughter as something that belongs to him, as property which is his to do with as he wishes. See Burgess et al., p. 22; Justice, p. 76. Interestingly, primitive societies associate incest with greed and selfishness, regarding it as a form of "antisocial and repellant hoarding"; the Arapesh equate the taking of one's sister or mother to the eating of one's own excess yams or pigs. See Mead, p. 83.

51. Authorities on incest note the isolation of incest offenders within society and within the family. Burgess et al.: "Themes of isolation and depression in incest are . . . frequent" (22); Justice: "Most of the incestuous fathers are inclined by personality to cut themselves off from others and become isolated. . . . The daughters, also, are characterized by a quality of loneliness" (135); Forward and Buck: "Family members are often emotionally isolated from one another and there is usually a good deal of loneliness and hostility before incest occurs" (4); Meiselman: "Weinberg (1955, p. 94) suggested that the term endogamic be used to describe a father who is an ingrown personality type . . . who confines his sexual objects to family members. . . . And clinical studies done after Weinberg's classification . . . have found endogamic characteristics in most or all of their subjects" (107–108).

52. The need to govern the appetites is a prominent theme in both Faulkner and Milton.

53. Faulkner, *Faulkner in the University,* p. 6.

54. Faulkner, *Essays, Speeches and Public Letters,* p. 137. Faulkner makes this point repeatedly, not only in his fiction and essays, but in interviews as well. See *Lion in the Garden,* pp. 56, 94, 125, 159, 206.

55. According to Charles Peavy, who finds corroboration in six different collections of Southern folklore,"the belief that jaybirds go to hell on Friday" is "widespread . . . throughout the South." See "Faulkner's Use of Folklore in *The Sound and the Fury,*" *Journal of American Folklore* 79 (1966): pp. 442–43.

56. For references in *Paradise Lost* to the "vacant room" and forlorn woods, see Milton II.835, VII.190, IX.148, 910. The use of Quentin's room as an emblem of a moral collapse is supported by the room's air of disorder, cheapness, tawdriness, anonymity, and decadence. Some critics, however, regard the empty room in a far different light. Carvel Collins writes, "Miss Quentin's empty room and abandoned lingerie have pointed relationship with Christ's empty tomb and discarded grave clothes." See "The Pairing," p. 117. Millgate, who sees Quentin as a force for life, says that "it is perhaps to be taken as a sign of hope—especially in view of the resurrection images which some critics have perceived in the description of her empty room—that Quentin finally makes good her escape and that, unlike her mother, she leaves no hostage behind." See Millgate, *The Achievment,* p. 103.

57. The image of the Eye also appears in *Soldier's Pay,* where it clearly refers to some heavenly body; as he lies on the grass, looking at the sky, George Farr comes to feel that he is disembodied, reduced to the function of sight, and transformed into "a bodiless Eye suspended in dark-blue space, an Eye without Thought" (236).

58. William Faulkner, "The Hill," in *William Faulkner: Early Prose and Poetry,* comp. and introd. Carvel Collins (Boston: Little, Brown, 1962), pp. 90–92.

59. William Faulkner, *Mayday,* introd. Carvel Collins (Notre Dame: University of Notre Dame Press, 1976), pp. 78–79. In *Soldier's Pay,* also, falling is fused with the act of love, in Januarius Jones' description of the mating of falcons: "They embrace at an enormous height and fall locked, beak to beak, plunging: an unbearable ecstasy" (227).

60. The interest in sex and death within the doctrine of the Fall is scarcely new; James Brain notes it in the writings of St. Paul, St. Augustine of Hippo, St. Thomas Aquinas, and Martin Luther (80).

61. Beverly Gross, "Form and Fulfillment in *The Sound and the Fury,*" *Modern Language*

Quarterly 29 (1968): 445; Joseph Gold, "Faulkner's *The Sound and the Fury*," *Explicator* 19 (1961): item 29; Millgate, *Achievment*, p. 103. Gross is right, I believe, in seeing this ending as an epitome of the novel but wrong in finding it "a symbolic situation with no immediate key to its symbolism" (449).

62. See Gross, p. 444. *As I Lay Dying* also concludes a journey to the cemetery with a scene of sound and fury in which brother is pitted against brother. As the two guards arrive to take Darl to Jackson, Dewey Dell and Jewel attack him, one "scratching and clawing at him," the other shouting, "Kill him. Kill the son of a bitch" (*AILD*, 227). However, in this novel's ending, where the family's survival is assured and a new journey commences, the positive note is sounded more strongly.

63. In their discussions of the significance of the narcissus, Lawrence Bowling and Lawrance Thompson both overlook Caddy. Bowling maintains that the flower represents not only Benjy's selfishness but also his need for love; Thompson believes that it stands for the self-love of Mrs. Compson, Jason, and Quentin, a suggestion with which Peavy seems to concur. See Bowling, p. 485; Peavy, "Faulkner's Use of Folklore," p. 439; Thompson, *William Faulkner: An Introduction and Interpretation*, (1963; 2nd ed. New York: Holt, Rinehart and Winston, 1967), pp. 48–49.

64. In the conclusion of "The Kingdom of God," another narcissus is "splinted" to ease the agony of another idiot: "Again the poor damaged thing held its head erect, and the loud sorrow went at once from the idiot's soul." William Faulkner, *William Faulkner: New Orleans Sketches*, ed. Carvel Collins (New York: Random House, 1968), p. 60.

65. Blotner, *Faulkner*, I, p. 578; Bleikasten, *The Most Splendid Failure*, p. 185; Collins, "The Interior Monologues," p. 79; Brooks, *The Yoknapatawpha Country*, p. 348; Walter J. Slatoff, *Quest for Failure: A Study of William Faulkner* (Ithaca, N. Y.: Cornell University Press, 1960), p. 157.

66. Victor Strandberg discusses very fully the principle of inversion in Faulkner, devoting to it an entire chapter in his book. See *A Faulkner Overview: Six Perspectives* (Port Washington, New York: Kennikat Press, 1981), pp. 3–13.

67. William Faulkner, *Go Down, Moses* (1942; rpt. New York: Modern Library-Random House, 1955), p. 326. All further references to this work appear in the text as *GDM*.

Chapter 4

1. In *Absalom, Absalom!* Faulkner also maintains the interest in multiple perspectives which began with the writing of *The Sound and the Fury*. In this novel too the narrators represent faculties from Milton's faculty psychology; Rosa typifies passion, Quentin and Shreve the imagination, and Mr. Compson the rational side of man.

2. Floyd C. Watkins argues, convincingly, that Judith's state of mind is best explained by Emily Dickinson's poem, "After Great Pain," which demonstrates that external appearances can be diametrically opposed to feelings that lie within. See *The Flesh and the Word: Eliot, Hemingway, Faulkner* (Nashville: Vanderbilt University Press, 1971), p. 227.

3. William Faulkner, *Absalom, Absalom!* (1936; rpt. New York: Random House, 1966), p. 359. All further references to this work appear in the text as *AA*. Shreve unwittingly bolsters Quentin's position when he likens Bon to a cat, an animal that Faulkner singles out in *The Reivers* for its refusal to care for anyone at all.

4. In selecting Drusilla as the name for a young woman with a propensity for incest, Faulkner may have had in mind the Roman Emperor Caligula's favorite sister—a woman notorious for her openly illicit relationship with her brother. See Suetonius, pp. 268–69. Melvin Backman notes that Drusilla is a Roman name but does not connect it with Caligula's sister (120).

5. William Faulkner, *The Unvanquished* (New York: Random House, 1938), p. 273. All further references to this work appear in the text as *Uv.*

6. William Bedford Clark, "The Serpent of Lust in the Southern Garden," *Southern Review* 10 (1974): 817-19.

7. "Elly" shares with the novel some notable similarities: the French origins of the man who is thought to be black; the fact that he comes from Louisiana; the murder of this young man; and the killing of a kinsman, in this case the old woman by her grand-daughter, Elly. See William Faulkner, "Elly," in *Collected Stories of William Faulkner* (1950; rpt. New York: Vintage-Random, 1977), pp. 207–224.

8. Clark, p. 809.

9. According to Cash, the veneration accorded the Southern woman resulted from the Southern man's guilt-ridden attempts to compensate for his faithlessness; the amount of the woman's suffering, he feels, can be measured by the extent of the idealization. See Wilbur J. Cash, *The Mind of the South* (New York: Alfred A. Knopf, 1941), pp. 84–86.

10. According to Faulkner, Bon "knew that if she [Judith] knew that he was part Negro, with her training and background it would have destroyed her too." See *Faulkner in the University,* p. 273.

11. In an earlier version of "Delta Autumn," written in 1940, no ties of kinship connect the mulatto woman and Don Boyd, who in *GDM* becomes Roth Edmonds. Similarly, in "Evangeline," a story written around 1931 which contains the seeds of *AA,* Judith and Charles are not related by blood. The inclusion of the incest in these relationships, however, adds greatly to their complexity and underscores the themes already intro-duced by the miscegenation. See William Faulkner, "Delta Autumn," in *Uncollected Stories of William Faulkner,* ed. Joseph Blotner (New York: Random House, 1979), pp. 267–80; William Faulkner, "Evangeline," in *Uncollected Stories,* pp. 583–609.

12. For a discussion of role violation in clinical studies of incest, see Justice, pp. 168–69; Kaufman, Peck, and Tagiuri, pp. 269–71; Meiselman, pp. 9, 126–30.

13. Young Isaac McCaslin in *Go Down, Moses* also experiences the lure of the mysterious black blood as he catches a glimpse of his uncle Hubert's light-skinned mistress, "an apparition rapid and tawdry and illicit yet somehow to the child, the infant still almost, breathless and exciting and evocative" (*GDM,* 302–303).

14. In his discussion of incest and miscegenation in Faulkner, Weatherby states that the incest is perceived as an alternative to miscegenation, that Henry "chooses Bon for Judith, almost sensing the blood link between them" (363). Jenkins believes that the Southern mentality equates incest with miscegenation, seeing both of them as a threat to "the sanctity of the bloodline." And he feels that the abhorrence with which the white man views miscegenation derives from the guilt of his own similar and repressed incestuous desires (56–57, 204–205).

15. For discussions of incest as the enemy of culture, see Fox, *Kinship and Marriage,* p. 56; Fox, *The Red Lamp,* pp. 11, 14; Brain, p. 41; Justice, p. 38; Potvin, pp. 420–21.

16. E. O. Hawkins suggests that Count John of Armagnac may have served as a source for Henry's duke. "Faulkner's 'Duke John of Lorraine,' " *American Notes and Queries* 4 (1965): 22.

17. For Lothar's story, see Duckett, pp. 34–39; McKeon, pp. 39–50; Simonde de Sismondi, pp. 343–49; Gwatkins et al., pp. 38–44.

18. A number of critics find significance in the names of Sutpen's children. Backman, Guerard and Irwin identify Judith with the Judith of the Old Testament, an identification which Irwin, oddly enough, regards as evidence that Judith Sutpen is a castrating female. Backman additionally links Bon with Bonnie Prince Charlie and associates Charles and Henry with English and Norman royalty, Clytemnestra with that of the Greeks; these names, he believes, reflect the dreams of their father. See Backman, pp. 100, 103, 104; Guerard, *The Triumph of the Novel,* p. 304; Irwin, pp. 50–51.

19. William Faulkner, *Knight's Gambit* (1949; rpt. New York: Vintage-Random, 1978), p. 143.

20. Faulkner, *Essays, Speeches and Public Letters,* p. 179.

21. Gerald Langford, *Faulkner's Revision of "Absalom, Absalom!": A Collation of the Manuscript and the Published Book* (Austin: University of Texas Press, 1971), pp. 19–20, 29, 32.

22. According to Vickery, Henry condones the incest because he sees in it evidence of a love "which will not be restricted." O'Conner interprets "this desire for incest" as "an acceptance of defeat and . . . doom," an acknowledgment of the "spiritual incest" already committed by the white people of the South in holding themselves apart from the black. See Vickery, p. 98; O'Conner, p. 98.

23. According to Kartiganer, Mr. Compson depicts "the attachment of Henry to Judith" as "the product of glands and conventional complexes" (83). Lensing maintains that Mr. Compson "intuits a love so rare and strong between the brother and sister that the metaphor which can best describe it is that of incest" (110). Both of these interpretations, I believe, are mistaken. While it consists of more than neurotic compulsions, this relationship can scarcely be designated as an ideal one.

24. The absence of a nurturing, supportive mother in the incestuous family is noted also in clinical studies. See Justice, p. 120; Kaufman, Peck, and Tagiuri, 269–71; Meiselman, pp. 127–29, 265.

25. In *The Golden Bough,* James Frazer points out that open doors were believed to facilitate the processes of both birth and death, man's entry into and egress from the world. See *The Golden Bough: A Study in Magic and Religion,* abr. ed. (1922; rpt. New York: MacMillan, 1951), pp. 279, 283.

26. Like doors, windows in Faulkner are often associated with sexual activities, but they point to something surreptitious in the relationship. Caddy's daughter and Rosa's aunt climb through windows to elope with, respectively, a carnival worker and a horse-and-mule trader; Joanna Burden for a week forces Joe Christmas, arriving nightly for the appointed tryst, to enter "the dark house" by way of the window.

27. Both Richard Adams and John Irwin feel that the homosexual attraction between

Henry and Bon is created by that which exists between Quentin and Shreve. This may be partially true; however, to see Henry's and Bon's relationship as merely a projection of Quentin's and Shreve's is to rob the Sutpen story of much of its significance. Nor does this theory take into account the fact that it is Mr. Compson, chiefly, who explores the peculiarities of this relationship between the Sutpen brothers. See Irwin, p. 78; Richard Adams, *Faulkner: Myth and Motion* (Princeton: Princeton University Press, 1968), p. 195.

28. Similarly, in *The Sound and the Fury* Caddy serves as an intermediary between Quentin and Ames; the two regard one another through Caddy, as though they were looking through colored glass. The role of the intermediary, however, is made even clearer in *The Hamlet,* where the school teacher Labove sees a fist fight with Jody Varner as a vicarious consummation of his love for Jody's sister, Eula: "That would be something, anyway. It would not be penetration, true enough, but it would be the same flesh . . . under impact at least—a paroxysm, an orgasm of sorts" (122).

Studies of incest offer several theories concerning incest's relationship to homosexuality: that homosexuality is the result or "symptom" of incest; that "one breeds the other"; that each is perceived as a defense against the other. See Forward and Buck, p. 163; Kaufman, Peck and Tagiuri, p. 277; Meiselman, pp. 215, 310; Santiago, p. 21.

29. This characterization of Henry very much agrees with W. J. Cash's concept of the young aristocrat in the Old South. In his attempt to describe the typical Southerner, Cash relies on Henry Adam's portrait of the Southern student at Harvard: a young man who had "no mind," only "temperament," who "was not a scholar," "had no intellectual training," and "could not analyze an idea." See Cash, p. 99.

30. Leslie Fiedler notes that Hawthorne's "Alice Doane's Appeal" "oddly resembles Faulkner's *Absalom, Absalom!,*" and he sees a parallel between "the struggle of Creole black and Puritan white brother" in *Absalom, Absalom!* and Hawthorne's "encounter of Old World and New World" in the persons of Walter Broame and his twin brother Leonard Doane (418–19).

Cash maintains that in the Southern psyche a Puritanical strain existed alongside a hedonistic love of pleasure but that the Puritanism predominated (57–58, 133–34).

31. Bon's propensity to use people is quite evident in "Evangeline," where the narrator speculates that Bon, who appeared to "be that sort of guy," had probably wrangled an invitation to Sutpen's Hundred from an unsuspecting Henry (586).

32. On the question of motive, the critics offer interpretations as varied as the narrators'. Bradford, who feels that Bon "probably 'needs killing,'" states that Henry kills Bon in order to protect the sister he loves. Jenkins believes that Henry is actually trying to kill "the nigger" in himself, that is, the dark desires that Bon represents. Irwin suggests that the murder of Bon is a reenactment of the oedipal drama, in which Henry plays the father who kills the son but also is the younger brother who kills the elder one, a surrogate for the father. See Melvin E. Bradford, "Brother, Son, and Heir: The Structural Focus of Faulkner's *Absalom, Absalom!,*" *Sewanee Review* 78 (1970): 80–83; Jenkins, p. 212; Irwin, pp. 49, 118.

33. Should incest prove to be the cause of Bon's death, it would only bear out what has been popularly believed for years—that incest always results in some form of catastrophe. Incest has been thought to cause "madness and death," natural disasters, "murders, suicides, and neurotic and psychotic breakdowns." See Thorslev, 45; Fox, *Red Lamp,* p. 6; Cory and Masters, p. 9.

34. Old Testament law forbids the marriage of a man with his sister-in-law: "Thou shalt not uncover the nakedness of thy brother's wife: it is thy brother's nakedness"; "And if a man shall take his brother's wife, it is an unclean thing: he hath uncovered his brother's nakedness; they shall be childless" (Lev. xviii.16 and xx.21). Church law also forbids such a marriage: in the Middle Ages, the Roman Catholic Church defined incest as "marriage within 'the fourth degree of kinship' "; today in England "marriage with a deceased wife's sister is not illegal or a crime but is a sin." See Justice, pp. 37, 39.

35. W. J. Cash has given the name of "the savage ideal" to this code in which violence is sanctioned, romanticism and hedonism encouraged, religion made prescriptive and repressive, and dissent is extinguished. See *The Mind of the South*, pp. 90, 91, 134, 135, 141.

36. The relationship between Rosa and Sutpen corresponds more closely to father-daughter incest than that of the brother and sister-in-law which it actually would be. Sutpen is old enough to be the father of Rosa, who is in fact four years younger than any of his children. Sutpen also fits, in a number of regards, the profile of the incestuous father which clinical studies provide: he is authoritarian; he exploits the young girl; he is himself emotionally impoverished. See Burgess et al., p. 22; Forward and Buck, p. 33; Justice, p. 76; Meiselman, pp. 86, 90.

37. William Faulkner, *Pylon* (1935; rpt. New York: Random House, 1965), p. 277.

38. It is possible that the redworm also refers to Sutpen, who not only has red hair and a red beard but is also identified with Satan, the "worm" of *Paradise Lost*.

39. Cleanth Brooks notes briefly the resemblance between Sutpen and Henry: "Not even Henry VIII wanted a son more intensely." "On *Absalom, Absalom!*," *Mosaic* 7 (1973): 178.

40. Scarisbrick, p. 371.

41. Dickens, p. 295.

42. Henry was "descended directly many times from Judith, the incestuous daughter of Charles the Bald." Santiago, p. 76.

43. Cleanth Brooks, "Faulkner and History," *Mississippi Quarterly* 25 (1972): 3.

44. In his description of Genghis, Caesar, William, Hitler, Barca, Bonaparte, Stalin, and Huey Long as "ambition's ruthless avatars," Faulkner makes very clear the prominence of ambition in the tyrant's make-up. See *Essays, Speeches and Public Letters*, p. 137.
    It is unquestionably Milton's version of Nimrod's story and not the biblical account to which Faulkner is indebted. Genesis states only that Nimrod was "a mighty hunter" and that "the beginning of his kingdom was Babel"; no mention at all is made of the Tower of Babel. See Gen. x.8–10.

45. In his description of the building of Pandemonium, Milton links this structure specifically with the Tower of Babel, one of man's "Monuments of Fame" (*PL* I.692–99).

46. This phrase reminds us that one of the chief torments Satan suffers is "the thought . . . of lost happiness," "the bitter memory / Of what he was" (*PL* I.54–55, IV.24–25).

47. A similar passage in *Flags in the Dust* describes the doom that shadows the Sartoris name: "For there is death in the sound of it, and a glamorous fatality, like silver

pennons downrushing at sunset, or a dying fall of horns along the road at Roncevaux."
See Faulkner, *Flags in the Dust*, p. 370.

48. Similarly, Red's coffin in *Sanctuary* is knocked from its bier and crashes to the floor, the coffin falling open and the corpse tumbling "slowly and sedately out" (*SOT*, 242). Fiedler, erroneously I believe, maintains that Sutpen "grows in stature as he struggles to achieve that grand design that brings only loneliness and madness and destruction to his children and himself" (473).

49. The existence of just such a relationship is proposed, in a most unconvincing article, by Sanford Pinsker, who suggests that Milly Jones is Sutpen's daughter as well as his mistress. Pinsker's thesis rests on the very shaky grounds of a possible correlation between the triangular relationship of Judith, Bon, and Henry and that of Sutpen, Wash and Milly. See "Thomas Sutpen and Milly Jones: A Note on Paternal Design in *Absalom, Absalom!*," *Notes on Modern American Literature* I (1976): item 6.

50. The concept of sin as contagion, which is illustrated by the metamorphosis of Satan's crew, is present also in *Absalom, Absalom!*; there Judith and Charles Etienne contract and eventually succumb to a disease—Yellow Fever—which is symbolic of the racial hatred that has infected and destroyed the South.

51. Rosa also bears a strong resemblence to Emily Grierson, a Sin-like character who quite literally embraces death. The correspondence of the two women may, in fact, be suggested by the short story's title: "A Rose for Emily."

52. Faulkner's working title for *Absalom, Absalom!*, "Dark House," may well have come from Satan's designation of Hell as "this dark and dismal house of pain." See Faulkner, *Selected Letters*, pp. 78–79; see also *PL* II.823. And as Faulkner tells us in the Appendix of *The Sound and the Fury*, the Compson house and the Sutpen mansion were "laid out by the same architect" (*SFA*, 407).

53. Faulkner also associates Bon with glitter when he characterizes Ellen's air castles, built on the very shaky foundation of Bon's future induction to the family, as "this bright glitter of delusion" and a "beam filled with a substanceless glitter of tinsel motes" (*AA*, 75, 76).

54. Another fall into life which appears as a segment of arrested time is Ike's introduction to the wilderness in *Go Down, Moses*; here too the sense of suspension is conveyed in the imagery of water, in visions of the "infinite waste" and the eternal sea.

55. In *The Hamlet* similar words are used to depict Eula Varner in her puberty. In an interpretation which may be correct, as far as it goes, but which fails to take into account the pervasiveness of the imagery of suspension in Faulkner, Karl Zink maintains that this "oblivious state of listening bemusement . . . relates directly to the obliviousness of Nature" and identifies women with nature. "Faulkner's Garden: Woman and the Immemorial Earth," *Modern Fiction Studies* 2 (1959): 144.

56. At the close of *Mayday* there appears a similar tree which is linked explicitly with death; as its leaves "whirled up in the air and spun about it," turning into birds, the tree became Saint Francis, saying "Little Sister Death." Faulkner, *Mayday*, p. 87.

57. Faulkner, "The Hill", pp. 91–92.

58. William Faulkner, "Nympholepsy," in *Uncollected Stories*, pp. 332–34.

59. Richard Adams quite rightly recognizes the importance of this "static moment of

contemplation" in "The Hill" and in "Twilight," a poetic version of the sketch; but he seems somewhat vague as to the nature of its significance. He concludes, finally, that it constitutes "some timeless realization of the quality of life" and that it will help the young man who "must live in a changing world" to "deal with tomorrows." The purpose of this suspension in time, Adams believes, remains the same in *Absalom, Absalom!* where Faulkner has managed to achieve artistically—through the medium of Sutpen's story—what he has tried to do in "Twilight" and "The Hill"; in the novel "he has frozen into one timeless moment of contemplation all that his characters have found important or significant in the history, legend, and myth of their civilization" ("Apprenticeship," 40, 199–200).

60.   Faulkner, *Lion in the Garden*, p. 253.

61.   " 'Art,' " Faulkner says, " 'is the salvation of mankind' "; its aim is "to uplift man's heart," to inspire and sustain him in his struggle to survive, to "turn" him "to heaven." See *Lion in the Garden*, pp. 71, 94, 177; *Essays, Speeches and Public Letters*, p. 181; *Faulkner in the University*, p. 61.

Selected Bibliography

Primary Sources

Works of Faulkner

Faulkner, William. *Absalom, Absalom!* 1936; rpt. New York: Random House, 1966.

_____. Appendix. *The Sound and the Fury*. 1946; rpt. New York: Modern Library-Random House, 1967, pp. 403–27.

_____. *As I Lay Dying*. 1930; rpt. New York: Random House, 1964.

_____. *Collected Stories of William Faulkner*. 1950; rpt. New York: Vintage-Random, 1977.

_____. *Essays, Speeches and Public Letters*. Ed. James B. Meriwether. New York: Random House, 1965.

_____. *Faulkner in the University: Class Conferences at the University of Virginia, 1957–58*. Ed. F. L. Gwynn and J. L. Blotner. Charlottesville: University Press of Virginia, 1959.

_____. *Faulkner's Revision of "Absalom, Absalom!": A Collation of the Manuscript and the Published Book*. Ed. Gerald Langsford. Austin: University of Texas Press, 1971.

_____. *Flags in the Dust*. Ed. Douglas Day. New York: Random House, 1973.

_____. *Go Down, Moses*. 1942; rpt. New York: Modern Library-Random House, 1955.

_____. *The Hamlet*. 1940; rpt. New York: Random House, 1964.

_____. "An Introduction for *The Sound and the Fury*." Ed. James B. Meriwether. *Southern Review* 8 (1972): 705–10.

_____. "An Introduction to *The Sound and the Fury*." In *A Faulkner Miscellany*. Ed. James B. Meriwether. Jackson: University Press of Mississippi, 1974, pp. 156–61.

_____. *Knight's Gambit*. 1949; rpt. New York: Vintage-Random, 1978.

_____. *Light in August*. 1932; rpt. New York: Random House, 1967.

_____. *Lion in the Garden: Interviews with William Faulkner, 1926-1962*. Ed. James B. Meriwether and Michael Millgate. 1968; rpt. Lincoln: University of Nebraska Press, 1980.

_____. *Mayday*. Introd. Carvel Collins. Notre Dame: University of Notre Dame Press, 1976.

_____. *Mosquitoes*. 1927; rpt. New York: Liveright, 1951.

_____. *Pylon*. 1935; rpt. New York: Random House, 1965.

_____. *Sanctuary*. 1931; rpt. New York: Vintage-Random, 1967.

_____. *Sanctuary: The Original Text*. Ed. Noel Polk. New York: Random House, 1981.

_____. *Sartoris*. 1929; rpt. New York: Signet, 1964.

_____. *Selected Letters of William Faulkner*. Ed. Joseph Blotner. 1977; rpt. New York: Vintage-Random, 1978.

_____. *Soldier's Pay*. 1926; rpt. New York: Liveright, 1951.

―――――. *The Sound and the Fury.* 1929; rpt. New York: Random House, 1966.

―――――. *Uncollected Stories of William Faulkner.* Ed. Joseph Blotner. New York: Random House, 1979.

―――――. *The Unvanquished.* New York: Random House, 1938.

―――――. *The Wild Palms.* 1939; rpt. New York: Random House, 1984.

―――――. *William Faulkner: Early Prose and Poetry.* Ed. Carvel Collins. Boston: Little, Brown, 1962.

―――――. *William Faulkner: New Orleans Sketches.* Ed. Carvel Collins. New York: Random House, 1968.

Works of Other Authors

Anderson, Sherwood. *Winesburg, Ohio.* 1919; rpt. New York: Penguin, 1976.

Mann, Thomas. *Death in Venice.* Trans. Kenneth Burke. New York: Alfred A. Knopf, 1925.

Maugham, W. Somerset. "Rain." In *East and West.* Vol. II of *The Complete Short Stories of W. Somerset Maugham.* Garden City, New York: Doubleday, 1934, pp. 1–39.

Milton, John. *Paradise Lost.* In *Complete Poems and Major Prose.* Ed. Merritt Y. Hughes. Indianapolis: The Odyssey Press, 1957, pp. 173–470.

Secondary Sources

Studies in Literature

Adams, Percy G. "Humor as Structure and Theme in Faulkner's Trilogy." *Wisconsin Studies in Contemporary Literature* 5 (1964): 205–12.

Adams, Richard P. "The Apprenticeship of William Faulkner." *Tulane Studies in English* 12 (1962): 113–56.

―――――. *Faulkner: Myth and Motion.* Princeton: Princeton University Press, 1968.

Aiken, David. "The 'Sojer Face' Defiance of Jason Compson." *Thought* 52 (1977): 188–203.

Arthos, John. "Ritual and Humor in the Writing of William Faulkner." *Accent* 9 (1948): 17–30.

Beckman, Melvin. *Faulkner: The Major Years.* Bloomington: Indiana University Press, 1966.

Bleikasten, Andre. *Faulkner's "As I Lay Dying."* Bloomington: Indiana University Press, 1973.

―――――. *The Most Splendid Failure: Faulkner's "The Sound and the Fury."* Bloomington: Indiana University Press, 1976.

Blotner, Joseph. *Faulkner: A Biography.* 2 vols. New York: Random House, 1974.

―――――. "William Faulkner's Essay on the Composition of *Sartoris.*" *The Yale University Library Gazette* 47 (1973): 121–24.

―――――. *William Faulkner's Library: A Catalogue.* Charlotesville: University Press of Virginia, 1964.

Bowling, Lawrence E. "Faulkner and the Theme of Innocence." *Kenyon Review* 20 (1958): 466–87.

Bradford, Melvin E. "Brother, Son, and Heir: The Structural Focus of Faulkner's *Absalom, Absalom!*" *Sewanee Review* 78 (1970): 76–98.

―――――. "Certain Ladies of Quality: Faulkner's View of Women and the Evidence of 'There was a Queen.' " *The Arlington Quarterly* 1 (1967-68): 106–39.

Brooks, Cleanth. "Faulkner and History." *Mississippi Quarterly* 25 (1972): 3–14.

―――――. "On *Absalom, Absalom!*" *Mosaic* 7 (1973): 159–83.

―――――. *William Faulkner: Toward Yoknapatawpha and Beyond.* New Haven: Yale University Press, 1978.

_____. *William Faulkner: The Yoknapatawpha Country.* 1963; rpt. New Haven: Yale University Press, 1977.

Brylowski, Walter. *Faulkner's Olympian Laugh: Myth in the Novels.* Detroit: Wayne State University Press, 1968.

Burch, Beth. "A Miltonic Echo in Faulkner's *The Hamlet.*" *Notes on Contemporary Literature,* 8, No. 4, n. d., 3–4.

Castille, Philip. " 'There Was a Queen' and Faulkner's Narcissa Sartoris." *Mississippi Quarterly* 28 (1975): 307–15.

Clark, William Bedford. "The Serpent of Lust in the Southern Garden." *Southern Review* 10 (1974): 805–22.

Coindreau, Maurice, traduction et preface. *Le Bruit et la fureur.* By William Faulkner. 1938; rpt. Paris: Gallimard, 1949.

Collins, Carvel. "The Interior Monologues of *The Sound and the Fury.*" In *English Institute Essays, 1952.* Ed. Alan Downer. New York: Columbia University Press, 1954. Rpt. in *The Merrill Studies in "The Sound and the Fury."* Ed. James B. Meriwether. Columbus, Ohio: Merrill, 1970, pp. 59–79.

_____. "Miss Quentin's Paternity Again." *Texas Studies in Language and Literature* 2 (1960): 253–260.

_____. "The Pairing of *The Sound and the Fury* and *As I Lay Dying.*" *Princeton University Library Chronicle* 18 (1957): 114–32.

Dauner, Louise. "Quentin and the Walking Shadow: The dilemma of Nature and Culture." *Arizona Quarterly* 21 (1965): 159–71.

Fiedler, Leslie A. *Love and Death in the American Novel.* 1960; rev. ed. New York: Stein and Day, 1966.

Gidley, Mich. "Some Notes on Faulkner's Reading." *Journal of American Studies* 4 (1970): 91–102.

Gold, Joseph. "Faulkner's *The Sound and the Fury.*" *Explicator* 19 (1961): item 29.

Gross, Beverly. "Form and Fulfillment in *The Sound and the Fury.*" *Modern Language Quarterly* 29 (1968): 439–49.

Guerard, Albert J. "The Faulknerian Voice." *The Maker and the Myth: Faulkner and Yoknapatawpha, 1977.* Ed. Evans Harrington and Ann J. Abadie. Jackson: University Press of Mississippi, 1978, pp. 25–42.

_____. *The Triumph of the Novel: Dickens, Dostoevsky, Faulkner.* New York: Oxford University Press, 1976.

Haury, Beth B. "The Influence of Robinson Jeffers' 'Tamar' on *Absalom, Absalom!*" *Mississippi Quarterly* 25 (1972): 356–58.

Hawkins, E. O. "Faulkner's 'Duke John of Lorraine.' " *American Notes and Queries* 4 (1965): 22.

Hopper, Vincent F. "Faulkner's *Paradise Lost.*" *Virginia Quarterly Review* 23 (1947): 405–20.

Howe, Irving. *William Faulkner: A Critical Study.* 1951; rpt. Chicago: University of Chicago Press, 1975.

Hunt, Joel. "Thomas Mann and Faulkner: Portrait of a Magician." *Wisconsin Studies in Contemporary Literature* 8 (1967): 431–36.

Hunt, John W. *William Faulkner: Art in Theological Tension.* Syracuse, N. Y.: Syracuse University Press, 1965.

Irwin, John T. *Doubling and Incest / Repetition and Revenge: A Speculative Reading of Faulkner.* Baltimore: The Johns Hopkins University Press, 1975.

Jacobs, Robert D. "Faulkner's Tragedy of Isolation." In *Southern Renascence: The Literature of the Modern South.* Ed. Louis D. Rubin, Jr. and Robert D. Jacobs. Baltimore: The John Hopkins University Press, 1953, pp. 170–91.

Jenkins, Lee. *Faulkner and Black-White Relations: A Psychoanalytic Approach.* New York: Columbia University Press, 1981.

Kartiganer, Donald M. *The Fragil Thread: The Meaning of Form in Faulkner's Novels.* Amherst: The University of Massachussetts Press, 1979.

Kloss, Robert J. "Faulkner's *As I Lay Dying,*" *American Imago* 38 (1981): 429–44.

Labor, Earle. "Faulkner's *The Sound and the Fury.*" *Explicator* 17 (1959): item 30.

Lawrence, David Herbert. "Edgar Allan Poe." In his *Studies in Classic American Literature.* New York: T. Seltzer, 1923. Rpt. in *The Recognition of Edgar Allan Poe: Selected Criticism since 1829.* Ed. Erle W. Carlson. Ann Arbor: University of Michigan Press, 1966, pp. 110–126.

Lensing, George S. "The Metaphor of Family in *Absalom, Absalom!*" *Southern Review* 11 (1975): 99–117.

Lytle, Andrew. "The Working Novelist and the Mythmaking Process." *Daedalus* 98 (1959): 326–38. Rpt. in *Myth and Literature: Contemporary Theory and Practice.* Ed. John B. Vickery. Lincoln: Bison-University of Nebraska Press, 1966, pp. 99–108.

McSweeny, Kerry. "The Subjective Intensities of Faulkner's *Flags in the Dust.*" *The Canadian Review of American Studies* 8 (1977): 154–64.

Millgate, Michael. *The Achievement of William Faulkner.* 1963; rpt. Lincoln: University of Nebraska Press, 1978.

————. "Faulkner's Masters." *Tulane Studies in English* 23 (1978): 143–55.

Minter, David. *William Faulkner: His Life and Work.* Baltimore: The Johns Hopkins University Press, 1980.

Morillo, Marvin. "Faulkner's *The Sound and the Fury.*" *Explicator* 24 (1966): item 50.

Morrison, Gail Moore. "Time, Tide, and Twilight: *Mayday* and Faulkner's Quest Toward *The Sound and the Fury.*" *Mississippi Quarterly* 31 (1978): 337–57.

O'Connor, William Van. *The Tangled Fire of William Faulkner.* 1954; rpt. New York: Gordian Press, 1968.

O'Donnell, George Marion. "Faulkner's Mythology." *The Kenyon Review* 1 (1939): 285–99. Rpt. in *Faulkner: A Collection of Critical Essays.* Ed. Robert Penn Warren. Englewood Cliffs, N.J.: Prentice-Hall, 1966, pp. 23–33.

Palliser, Charles. "Fate and Madness: The Determinist Vision of Darl Bundren." *American Literature* 49 (1978): 619–33.

Peavy, Charles D. " 'Did You Ever Have a Sister?'—Holden, Quentin, and Sexual Innocence." *Florida Quarterly* 1 (1968): 82–95.

————. "Faulkner's Use of Folklore in *The Sound and the Fury.*" *Journal of American Folklore* 79 (1966): 437–47.

Pinsker, Sanford. "Thomas Sutpen and Milly Jones: A Note on Paternal Design in *Absalom, Absalom!*" *Notes on Modern American Liturature* 1 (1976): item 6.

Seltzer, Leon F. "Narrative Function vs. Psychopathology: The Problem of Darl in *As I Lay Dying.*" *Literature and Psychology* 25 (1975): 49–64.

Simpson, Lewis P. "Faulkner and the Legend of the Artist." In *Faulkner: Fifty Years after "The Marble Faun."* Ed. George H. Wolfe. Tuscaloosa: University of Alabama Press, 1976, pp. 69–100.

————. "Sex and History: Origins of Faulkner's Apocrypha." In *The Maker and the Myth: Faulkner and Yoknapatawpha, 1977.* Ed. Evans Harrington and Ann J. Abadie. Jackson: University Press of Mississippi, 1978, pp. 43–70.

Slatoff, Walter J. *Quest for Failure: A Study of William Faulkner.* Ithaca, N. Y.: Cornell University Press, 1960.

Spilka, Mark. "Quentin Compson's Universal Grief." *Contemporary Literature* 2 (1970): 451–69.

Strandberg, Victor. *A Faulkner Overview: Six Perspectives.* Port Washington, New York: Kennikat Press, 1981.

Swiggart, Peter. "Moral and Temporal Order in *The Sound and the Fury.*" *Sewanee Review* 61 (1953): 221–37.

Tate, Allen. "Our Cousin, Mr. Poe." Poe Society of Baltimore. 7 October 1949; rpt. in *Poe: A Collection of Critical Essays.* Ed. Robert Regan. Englewood Cliffs, N.J.: Prentice-Hall, 1967, pp. 38–50.

Thompson, Lawrance. *William Faulkner: An Introduction and Interpretation.* New York: Barnes and Noble, 1963.

Thorslev, Peter L., Jr. "Incest as Romantic Symbol." *Comparative Literature Studies* 2 (1965): 41–58.

Vickery, Olga. *The Novels of William Faulkner: A Critical Interpretation.* 1959; rev. ed. Baton Rouge: Louisiana State University Press, 1964.

Waggoner, Hyatt. *William Faulkner: From Jefferson to the World.* Lexington: University of Kentucky Press, 1959.

Wasson, Ben. *Count No 'Count: Flashbacks to Faulkner.* Jackson: University Press of Mississippi, 1983.

Watkins, Floyd C. *The Flesh and the Word: Eliot, Hemingway, Faulkner.* Nashville: Vanderbilt University Press, 1971.

Weatherby, H. L. "Sutpen's Garden." *Georgia Review* 21 (1967); 354–69.

Ziegfeld, Richard Evan. "A Methodology for the Study of Philosophy in Literature: Philosophy and Symbol in Selected Works of William Faulkner and Thomas Mann." Diss. University of Texas, 1976.

Zink, Karl. "Faulkner's Garden: Woman and the Immemorial Earth." *Modern Fiction Studies* 2 (1959): 139–49.

Studies in Other Disciplines

Brain, James. *The Last Taboo: Sex and the Fear of Death.* Garden City, N.Y.: Anchor-Doubleday, 1979.

Burgess, Ann W. et al. *Sexual Assault of Children and Adolescents.* Toronto: D. C. Heath, 1978.

Cash, Wilbur J. *The Mind of the South.* New York: Alfred A. Knopf, 1941.

Cory, Donald W. and Masters, R. E. L. *Violation of Taboo: Incest in the Great Literature of the Past and Present.* New York: The Julian Press, 1963.

Davis, J. J. "Incest (in the Bible)." In *New Catholic Encyclopedia,* VII, pp. 419–20.

Dickens, Arthur G. *The English Reformation.* New York: Schocken Books, 1964.

Duckett, Eleanor S. *Alfred the Great.* Chicago: The University of Chicago Press, 1956.

Forward, Susan and Buck, Craig. *Betrayal of Innocence: Incest and its Devastation.* Los Angeles: J. P. Tarcher, 1978.

Fox, Robin. *Kinship and Marriage: An Anthropological Perspective.* Baltimore: Penguin, 1967.

————. *The Red Lamp of Incest.* New York: E. P. Dutton, 1980.

Frazer, James. *The Golden Bough: A Study in Magic and Religion.* Abr. ed. 1922; rpt. New York: Macmillan, 1951.

Freud, Sigmund. *Totem and Taboo: Resemblances between the Psychic Lives of Savages and Neurotics.* Trans. and introd. A. A. Brill. New York: Moffat, Yard, 1918.

Fromm, Eric. *The Sane Society.* New York: Rinehart, 1955.

Gwatkin, H. et al. *Germany and the Western Empire.* Vol. III of *The Cambridge Medieval History.* New York: Macmillan, 1922, pp. 38–46.

Justice, Blair and Rita. *The Broken Taboo: Sex in the Family.* New York: Human Sciences Press, 1979.

Kaufman, Irving; Peck, Alice; and Tagiuri, Consuelo. "The Family Constellation and Overt Incestuous Relations between Father and Daughter." *American Journal of Orthopsychiatry,* 24 (1954), pp. 266–79.

Masters, William and Johnson, Virginia. "Incest: The Ultimate Sexual Taboo." *Redbook,* April 1976, pp. 54–58.

May, Rollo. *Man's Search for Himself.* 1953; rpt. New York: Dell, 1980.

McKeon, Peter R. *Hincmar of Laon and Carolingian Politics.* Urbana: University of Illinois Press, 1978.

Mead, Margaret. *Sex and Temperament in Three Primitive Societies.* New York: William Morrow, 1935.

Meiselman, Karin C. *Incest: A Psychological Study of Causes and Effects with Treatment Recommendations.* San Francisco: Jossey-Bass, 1978.

Potvin, R. H. "Incest Taboo." In *New Catholic Encyclopedia,* VII, pp. 420–21.

Puckett, Newbell Niles. *Folks Beliefs of the Southern Negro.* Chapel Hill: North Carolina University Press, 1926.

Santiago, Luciano P. R. *The Children of Oedipus: Brother-Sister Incest in Psychiatry, Literature, History, and Mythology.* Roslyn Heights, N. Y.: Libra Publishers, 1973.

Scarisbrick, J. J. *Henry VIII.* Berkeley: University of California Press, 1968.

Simonde de Sismondi, J. C. L. *The French under the Merovingians.* Trans. William Bellingham. London, 1850; rpt. New York: AMS Press, 1976.

Suetonius, C. Tranquillas. *The Lives of the Twelve Caesars.* Trans. Alexander Thomson. 1796; rev. T. Forester. London: George Bell and Sons, 1890.

Index